NATURALIST IN TWO WORLDS

NATURALIST IN TWO WORLDS

Random Recollections
of a University President

by Alexander G. Ruthven

Ann Arbor
The University of Michigan Press

DEDICATION   To you who for many years have stood beside and behind me this little book is respectfully dedicated. You have held my hand in sorrow, encouraged me in trying times, often kept me out of trouble with your advice, and, most important of all, laughed with me on all proper, and some improper, occasions. Together we have managed to be reasonably happy while assisting a great university to weather a period in its history in which it was severely buffeted by the storms of war, financial depression, and social change. For all of this, my heartfelt thanks.

Alexander G. Ruthven

FOR TEN YEARS I have been importuned by friends to compile my memoirs. I have resisted for what I have considered good reasons. Biographies leave me with a feeling of frustration. When I read one I am aware that much knowledge of human affairs lies buried in the minds of dead men. I am also prone to recall a statement of Channing: "Most biographies are of little worth —they are panegyrics not lives."

I also lack confidence in autobiographies. It is too much to expect that these productions can be uncolored or entirely objective—human nature being what it is.

I have finally compromised by compiling a sketch, noting some conclusions I have reached, and recalling experiences which have influenced my thinking and actions as a university president. I assume it to be true that "an episode is worth a volume of biography."

For the most part I have omitted names and specific dates. I could not possibly give adequate credit to all of those to whom I have become indebted. Also I have wanted to avoid a detailed chronology; this responsibility I bequeath to some future historian of the University of Michigan.

I have used the word "naturalist" in the title of this account of my career because I believe that my training as a biologist has influenced my view of life and its problems and consequently many of my decisions as a college administrator.

Contents

Adaptation

*Just as the twig is bent, the
tree is inclined.*

BEGINNINGS

SINCE THE INCIDENT of my birth, on an April Fools' Day
somewhere in northwestern Iowa, I have had six rebirths. My
boyhood was spent in the small Iowa town bearing the family
name, with father, mother, a brother, a sister, and grand-
parents, aunts, uncles, and cousins of the Ruthven clan.

I consider that my life began in a real sense when I was between nine and twelve years old, when I discovered an absorbing interest in nature. I spent all the time I could, outside of
school hours, tramping or riding my cow pony over the open
prairies of northwestern Iowa. The only natural history book I
had was a *Woods Natural History*. In the evenings I pored over
it, trying to identify as well as possible the animals with which
I was becoming familiar.

A remarkable event occurred when I was twelve years old
which I cannot fully explain. I mentioned in my mother's hearing one day that I would like to have a copy of a book I had
heard about, the *Origin of Species* by Darwin. Much to my
surprise I received a copy as a Christmas present. My mother
was a disciplinarian with a strict code of ethics, but apparently
she was not a fundamentalist. At that time not only his book
but the very name of Charles Darwin was anathema to most
churchgoers.

Darwin's epoch-making work is hard going even for an
adult, but I absorbed the contents of every page, even though

I had to read some pages many times. From then on I knew I must, if possible, become a biologist of some kind. The height of my ambition as a boy was to study in a museum or zoological garden.

My Scottish grandmother was a Presbyterian who firmly believed in predestination. In fact she did not hesitate on appropriate occasions to tell her sons which ones were going to heaven and which to everlasting torment. When I was eight or nine my mother had the bumps on my head examined by a phrenologist. I don't remember what he discovered as to my future, but my grandmother was disgusted with such nonsense and told me that I was foreordained to be a preacher or a teacher. At that time I could not have been less concerned, for my main interest outside of school was to be about the stables, herding cattle on the prairie, breaking horses, and learning all I could about the wild animals of all lands.

After finishing the eleventh-grade school at Ruthven, Iowa, I was shipped off to Morningside College, outside of Sioux City, a year later and admitted to the preparatory course. The shock of the environmental change was great, but I was never homesick because, I am sure, of my curiosity, my interest in reading, and my courses in biology.

UNDERGRADUATE LIFE

My second rebirth came when I enrolled in the preparatory school of my college. Here in my first year I became acquainted with one of the most inspiring teachers I have ever known. R. B. Wylie was then professor of botany in the college and a fellow in the University of Chicago. Shortly after I began my studies he offered me the position of voluntary assistant in his laboratory. No post I have since held has given me a greater feeling of pride. I was able to keep this post through my undergraduate years.

Professor Wylie taught his students two important lessons

—in addition to biological facts and principles. He insisted that regardless of their interests or chosen field they should secure a broad education. He also urged them to realize the importance of being tactful without being evasive when their controversial subject was under discussion by laymen. The latter was a very important lesson in those days, particularly in church schools. After Darwin, in the popular mind, all evolutionists were atheists who believed that man was simply a monkey without a caudal appendage. Teachers of biology were considered as subversive as communists came to be in later years.

Under the almost daily guidance of Wylie and his successor, T. C. Frye, I took my first steps toward a career in science. In this period I came to appreciate the saying of Alexander of Macedon: "I am indebted to my father for living, but to my teacher for living well." Aristotle could not have wished for a more rewarding accolade.

College life at Morningside was a pleasant and rewarding experience. The student body was small, and everyone knew everyone. My professors were the heads of their departments. The college was several miles from town, and there were, of course, no movie houses, beer parlors, radios, or television sets, and few telephones. We arranged our own entertainments. The only athletics was a student-managed football team, on which I played for a time. Social activities were grouped about the literary clubs.

This will seem dull to the modern college student. We did not find it so. At any rate we had ample time to study, and we in the sciences particularly enjoyed the opportunities given us to spend extra hours in the laboratories working side by side with our professors.

UNIVERSITY SPECIALIZATION

My third beginning really occurred a year before I graduated from college, when R. B. Wylie asked me to attend a summer quarter at the University of Chicago with him. He expected at that time that I would be a botanist and so did I. During this summer I had the great advantage of becoming personally acquainted with such distinguished scientists as Cowles, Whitman, Tower, Williston, and Coulter, and in particular with Charles C. Adams. Through a course with Adams I was introduced to the related fields of animal ecology and zoogeography. These were to be my areas of study during my scientific career.

I returned to college to receive the bachelor's degree the next year, inspired by the promise of a scholarship at Chicago after I had graduated.

While waiting to begin work at Chicago I was astonished to receive a telegram from Adams stating that he had joined the staff of the University of Michigan as curator of the University Museum, then a part of the Department of Zoology, and offering me an assistantship in the department if I cared to continue my graduate work with him. I accepted his invitation promptly, whereupon he asked me to come immediately to Michigan and to proceed to the Upper Peninsula of the state to join a geological survey field party in the Porcupine Mountains. I was to investigate the fauna of the region.

From this time on I worked for the doctorate at Michigan, serving as laboratory assistant in zoology and doing research in the Museum.

I came to Michigan as an assistant at a financial sacrifice. The University of Chicago scholarship in zoology carried an annual stipend of two hundred dollars. The rate at Michigan for assistants was somewhat lower—one hundred fifty dollars a year.

My duties at Michigan were laboratory teaching and the preparation of teaching materials. The latter activity included in one semester the touring of local farms on foot to secure cats for the comparative anatomy course. For a period I also collected earthworms at night in President Angell's garden and in the "wee small hours" prepared them for class study.

President James B. Angell must have been a sound sleeper, for he seemed never to be disturbed by my wanderings through his garden with my dark lantern in search of the wary Lumbricus. I was often accompanied in this pursuit by a talkative night watchman. Assistants worked late at night. It was necessary. Reuben, the watchman, often kept us company. He liked grog, but could be trusted not to drink the alcohol in which the specimens were preserved—a habit not unknown among museum and laboratory caretakers in those days.

Teaching assistants today tell me I am old-fashioned. When embalmed anatomical specimens, microscopic slides, dissections, and other laboratory materials are purchased from supply houses or prepared by technicians, and libraries can be called upon to provide bibliographies, many of the tasks we performed are considered menial and a waste of time. This may be true in part (I never could properly sharpen a microtome knife), but it should be helpful to the zoologist to be familiar with the tools and methods of his profession through their use. At any rate we were required to demonstrate some facility in operating microtomes and incubators, in staining and mounting sections, in making dissections, and in other laboratory techniques. No excuse was acceptable for not knowing the literature.

Adams was a fiery individual, very loyal to his serious students but impatient with others, and a hard taskmaster. He insisted that his students should read continuously, collect books in their field, work out their own bibliographies, and pursue their researches with all diligence. He frowned upon any real interest in sports or social activities. He insisted that the only exercise a student needed was to take a walk when he found that he was not thinking clearly.

As we knew him at Michigan, Adams was apparently a confirmed bachelor. Later he fell from grace. He was always opposed to young scientists taking on family obligations. When he learned I was contemplating marriage after finishing graduate work he warned me that if this occurred I should be unable to conduct the expeditions I had planned. His predictions did not come true—because when I told my bride-to-be how my chief felt she vowed that she would prove him wrong whatever inconveniences or sacrifices might result.

I had selected herpetology as my undergraduate field of study. The Reptilia had engaged the attention of distinguished scientists, but no one had applied the principles of geography and ecology to the solution of confusing problems of taxonomy and distribution.

As tools for my studies and as an avocation I collected during this time a large library of books and reprints on natural history. On my retirement the rare old editions were presented to the General Library of the University to be housed in the Rare Book Room. The modern works and reprints were deposited in the Museum of Zoology.

One of my chores as a laboratory assistant was the operation of the lantern for the lectures of the professors. These machines were equipped with an arc lamp, and it was a tricky job to keep the carbons adjusted. When they sputtered and went out, as occasionally happened, the lecturer could usually think of a sarcastic remark calculated to embarrass the assistant and amuse the students. In one of the classes I was particularly annoyed by a coed who sat near the lantern. When I was in trouble she would look my way and grin at my discomfiture. I finally got even with her—I married her.

During my student days at Michigan I gained an understanding of museums of zoology as scientific institutions. The need for materials for my thesis required visits to several large museums and loans of specimens from others. I learned from these experiences that a museum of zoology at its best is not a "dead circus," not a gallery of elaborate exhibits to astound the public, and not a storehouse of demonstration material for professors and students to tear to pieces. It is a teaching and research institution akin to a library. Its proper function is to gather intelligently and to preserve carefully specimens for research and to maintain exhibits illustrating biological facts and principles.

When Adams came to Michigan the University Museum was a hodgepodge of old exhibits and a few inadequate research collections. The staff consisted of a curator, a secretary, and a taxidermist. Each time the curator took a requisition to the Business Office the veteran secretary of the University would growl: "When is the Museum going to be finished?" He always received the same reply. Adams would snap back: "A finished museum is a dead museum."

In my time as a graduate student the emphasis in teaching was on embryology and morphology. My interest in ecology, geography, and variation, and my selection of the reptiles as a group to provide study materials attracted attention both in and out of the department. When President Angell enrolled me as a graduate student he evidently was impressed with the subject of my proposed thesis—the genetic relationships of the garter snakes. For years afterward, whenever we met on the campus he would raise his cane and greet me. "Good morning, Ruthven. How are the snakes?"

Adams' final responsibility at Michigan was to present me to the secretary of the University. The introduction was made when I submitted my first requisition. It was not propitious. These two men never agreed on much of anything.

"Mr. Secretary, this is my successor as curator of the University Museum."

"Does he know, Adams, that I think the Museum should be finished by this time and that we don't need a curator?"

"Oh, yes, I told him and he laughed."

"I suppose, like you Adams, he believes with Osler that some of us have lived too long?"

"I have not heard him say, Mr. Secretary, but I am sometimes quite sure that Osler is right."

My academic performance as a student will forever be a secret. In afteryears to prod my children to do well in school I could boast of a perfect record. Both my offspring and my secretary were skeptical. When they connived to check my class records, however, they were disappointed to discover there were none extant. My high school had burned. My college records had been destroyed by fire. I had been admitted to Michigan on diploma, and in my time graduate students were not graded on classwork—they passed or flunked. I cannot prove I was always a model student, but no one can prove I was not.

TEACHING AND RESEARCH

What I consider to have been a fourth start began the year I graduated at Michigan. Adams left for another post, and I was made curator of the Museum and instructor in zoology. The period following my appointment to the staff was in many respects one of the most pleasant and rewarding parts of my life. My teaching was practically limited to the instruction of graduate students, and I was able to carry on research with little interference. This was unusual, for at Michigan at that time the teaching staff was supposedly paid to teach. Research was not frowned upon, but it was to be carried on in one's "spare time." Facilities for investigations were meager, and publication by the University was only possible at the expense of interested patrons. One of the presidents under whom I served often tried to "encourage" the faculty by pointing out that many great discoveries had been made in attics by underpaid professors with "make it yourself" equipment! This was little encouragement.

One instructor was heard to comment: "Perhaps if the President lived in an attic he could get a broader view of what the University should be about."

During this period I organized and directed biological expeditions to various parts of the United States, Middle America, South America, and the islands of the Caribbean. I became acquainted both personally and through letters with distinguished scholars in the United States, Great Britain, and Germany. It was a painful wrench when I was induced, if not compelled, to exchange this "birthright" for what some of my friends called a "mess of pottage."

There were two schools of thought on the campus in regard to our expeditions. Some thought that each year we were engaging in a dangerous enterprise. Another group seemed to think we were having a vacation. Of course the work was not really dangerous. The members of our parties were probably safer in the jungles and on the deserts than they would have been in some cities. We did, however, have some interesting experiences not only in our scientific activities but also incidentally.

It seemed to happen more often than not that when we were ready to return from the field we acquired some zoological specimens which we did not have time to preserve. These, if important, we endeavored to bring back alive to Ann Arbor. On an expedition to southern Vera Cruz the Indians brought in two boa constrictors about ten or eleven feet long just before our departure. We placed them in a suitcase in our stateroom. During the voyage home it became quite cold, and we feared the boas would not live to reach Ann Arbor. Mrs. Ruthven, who accompanied us on this trip, solved the problem. She placed them in two cheesecloth bags and put them in her berth. All three got along very comfortably. To this day alumnae often shudder and wonder how she could have such devotion to science. I have reminded them that she specialized in zoology, that the snakes were quite harmless, and that no self-respecting boa would be interested in swallowing anything as "skinny" as she was.

This episode had an aftermath. In our travels we always had an impressive letter from the University with a gold seal and ribbons which, like other explorers, we called "dago dazzlers." We also had documents from the Department of State requesting customs officials to allow us to enter American ports without the ordeal of having our baggage examined. On this occasion, however, we encountered a tough customs official in New York who was not impressed either by the University of Michigan or the State Department. He insisted that we open all of our fourteen cases. Fortunately, as it turned out, my young assistant—later a professor of zoology in another university—had an inspiration. He turned to me and said, "Chief, I'll open the chests but this guy can help us with the suitcases." Whereupon he handed the inspector the bag with the boas. The official jerked open the case, gave a gasp, slammed it shut, and asked in a trembling voice, "How many of these things do you have?" Somewhat evasively I said, "We probably have some 12,000 specimens." Of course they were not all snakes and they were not all alive. He turned to me and snapped, "I want you men to get this stuff off this dock immediately. If you open one chest I will have you arrested." There was no delay.

We were working in the swamps and jungles up the Demerara River in British Guiana. I was anxious to get a good series for the University of the very venomous bushmaster. Some fine specimens of this snake in Guiana reach a length of ten or eleven feet. They were, however, not easy to find, and I engaged some Indians to help us. Very soon we were disturbed to find that the natives were coming into camp with these reptiles alive. Since they knew how venomous they were it seemed to me that they were unduly careless in handling them. I feared if one of the hunters was killed our prestige would be seriously damaged. When I argued with them, however, they paid little attention, replying that they knew we had "snake medicine," which of course we did not. Fortunately, nothing happened.

Just before we left the field my assistant, with a perverted sense of humor, suggested that we stop collecting and dismiss our aides with the exception of one on whom we had come to place considerable reliance. He also suggested that we send this man into the field, with the bottle of brandy we had—which we were cherishing for medicinal purposes—and when he came back show him that he had been carrying liquor all day instead of medicine. It was, of course, a foolish thing to do, but we had few amusements, and it seemed funny at the time. When this man returned in the afternoon I was sweating out a spell of malaria in my hammock, not interested in much of anything. I noticed, however, that he seemed to be unusually talkative and pleasant. I asked him for the bottle and specimens. Whereupon he gave this account: He had been resting on the shore of a small creek in the forest several miles from camp when he looked about and saw a big bushmaster approaching. Although he had no time to run, he feared naught. He took out the bottle of "snake medicine," drank the contents, and then felt so safe that he turned and killed the snake with the bottle. I asked him for the snake. He again was prepared. He had cut it up so badly that he knew it was not any good as a specimen. The joke was on us. (Only one person knows to what extent this tale—which always amused the alumni—is apocryphal.)

Biologists will understand that I felt I was not in real danger when a poisonous snake slithered out of the bag I was holding and crawled up my sleeve or when I found I was being trailed for at least half a day by a large jaguar. I learned early, as do all naturalists, that few wild animals are dangerous unless they are wounded or have been persecuted. We never had a serious accident in our field work. I was twice, however, in some danger, and one of the perils, I am assured, hangs over my head to this day.

While we camped for a time in a tiny village in Colombia, with a native woman as our cook, the available water supply was a large swamp nearby. As biologists we knew that the water would be rich in proteins, and we preferred them cooked. We thought that the cook was carefully instructed to boil the drinking supply, and we were pleased to notice that she always had a pot on or near the fire. It was not until our last day in camp that we discovered she had thought it was sufficient to keep the water lukewarm for an hour or so. We must have been well supplied with vitamins.

While in the beautiful Santa Marta Mountains in Colombia we stayed for some weeks at a coffee hacienda in the jungle. It was at an altitude of about 5,000 feet on the mountain of San Lorenzo. While in the locality I was anxious to study the animal life above timberline, and three of us with a muleteer arranged a trip to the summit of San Lorenzo. All went well until, just before we started, a mysterious German count and countess appeared who insisted on accompanying us. Two things we did not need on this trip were a German count and countess, but we had to be polite, for they had been sent to the hacienda by some government agency. We capitulated after an argument and took them with us.

We reached the summit of San Lorenzo after a stiff climb above the spot where we left our mules. As it was late and getting cold when we arrived at the summit, we set up a canvas lean-to, built a fire, had supper, and rolled ourselves in blankets under the protection of the shelter. The next morning when I awakened I saw the men in the party standing in front of the lean-to with a camera taking a picture of the countess and me sleeping the sleep of the just. I have tried to buy or steal this picture for years without success. My companions claim to be holding it for blackmail on some appropriate occasion. I have tried to explain the whole occasion many times to Mrs. Ruthven, but all she will say is: "Well, sometime let me see the picture."

These trips were far from being picnics, for we were anxious to accomplish as much as possible in the available time. On almost every expedition in the tropics we were unable to avoid malaria, the work was done in the rainy season, and we depended for food largely on the animals we collected or could get from the natives. I vividly recall the time when my assistant and I had a dugout stuck in the mud of a creek in the low jungles far up the Demerara River. It was very hot and fast getting dark. The insects were pestering us, and the dugout seemed to weigh a ton. I looked at my assistant who was standing waist deep in the mud, his face covered with mosquitoes, and his clothes soaked with perspiration. He looked up, grinned, and said, "I wish to hell Dean E. was here." The dean was always saying how he envied us our summer vacations.

We were about to close our field season on the Demerara when two black boys appeared at camp. They informed us we were to leave the country at once and all arrangements had been made. Inquiring as to the reason, we were told that Germany and England had begun what later became known as World War I.

We could scarcely credit the news, but as the boys wore straw hats with "River Police" printed on the bands we concluded our packing, loaded a large dugout, and with a native crew departed for Georgetown. We were met by a somewhat hurt and irritated American consul. He had been rebuked by the State Department for not knowing we were in Guiana and had experienced difficulty in finding us. There *was* a war. The Germans were sinking British shipping, and the British were trying to capture the cargo vessels supplying a German raider, the "Dresden." On our way down we had met this ship sailing, according to her captain, under sealed orders.

We were told by the State Department to embark on a freighter bound for New York or to take the chance of staying in Guiana for the duration of the war. We left Georgetown in the middle of the night, the only passengers on a blacked-out ship. The captain was more concerned about running into native craft than of encountering the "Dresden." The next morning a speeding destroyer appeared in the distance, evidently bearing down on us. Passengers and crew were perturbed, the passengers principally over the possible loss of the fruits of their summer's work. Everyone relaxed when the destroyer "Berwick" slipped by, the band on her deck playing "America" (or so the mate said). After several delays we reached New York, our collections intact, thanks to Mrs. Ruthven, the University authorities, the future Senator Vandenberg, and Secretary of State William Jennings Bryan.

On many of my field trips I was accompanied by an assistant to whom I was indebted for aid in sickness and in health. On more than one occasion he saved my life.

After I became President of the University, except for a summer's work in Utah, I was in the field but once. When we were finishing our archeological explorations of Kôm Aushim on the edge of the oasis of Fayoum in the Sahara, Mrs. Ruthven and I visited the University's camp, which had been in operation for years, to see the work completed and to consult with the director about the possible selection of another site.

On departing for Egypt our scholars gave me a copy of one of our reports on this "dig," suitably inscribed to His Majesty King Fuad. I was to give the book to our minister to

Egypt, who would present it to the lord chamberlain for the royal library. I was very jealous of my time, but I felt I could do this without much inconvenience.

Immediately on arrival in Cairo we called on the minister, gave him the book, and departed for camp. After a few delightful days in the field a courier arrived by camel with the information that His Majesty requested an interview. This was an unwelcome interruption, but there was nothing to do but accede. With the director and my son, who was working in the camp that year, I went to Cairo the day before the audience was to be held, thinking this was time enough to make any necessary preparations. Being asked if I had the proper clothes I informed His Majesty's representative that I understood an audience at the Egyptian Court, as in other Eastern courts, regardless of the time of day, required evening dress. Much to my consternation, however, I was informed that the rules had been changed. I needed a frock coat, striped trousers, and a silk hat. I had not seen a frock coat for years except as pictured on a certain tobacco can. After much running about Cairo we found a tailor who was making a coat for a fat pasha. He agreed that before morning he would have this garment temporarily altered so that I could borrow it—for a consideration.

Properly garbed, I was ready for the King's car when it came for me. I soon discovered I was not to be received at the official palace in Cairo but at the residential palace in the suburbs, where I was met by the lord chamberlain and the American minister. To my surprise the lord chamberlain had the book I had brought for the royal library. I asked him to give the book to the library, but he said, "His Majesty insists on receiving it from your hand." I was a little overwhelmed, especially when the lord chamberlain opened the door for me to go in alone. Before he left me he murmured in my ear: "The interview will be about twelve minutes." I whispered in reply: "This will be longer than I need. I am accustomed to meeting queens

[on the Michigan campus] but I have not met a king before."
He did not seem to grasp my foolish remark.

I went down the long room full of chairs and ottomans to
the other end to be greeted by His Majesty. King Fuad knew
but would not speak English. I could understand his French
but refused to inflict my French on him. He called an interpreter
who soon retired. We couldn't be bothered with him. I spoke
English; the King French. We had, for me, an interesting discussion lasting almost an hour. I was amazed to find that His
Majesty had personal knowledge of our work in Egypt as well
as of the work of other expeditions. He knew the names of our
scholars, although he had not met them personally. I was so
interested in his remarks that when he terminated the interview
I backed down the long room making my three bows without
falling over a footstool!

In the afternoon following the interview, as I was entering
the hotel, the minister of education, the head of the Coptic
Church, and two other distinguished Arabs were having tea on
the terrace and motioned me to join them. They asked me how
I had gotten along. I waxed eloquent in my appreciation of the
King, his knowledge of our work, and the invitation he had
given Mrs. Ruthven and me to visit the tomb of his ancestors,
which was being readied for the services marking the end of
Ramadan. As they did not seem to be as impressed as I was
with my reception I enlarged on the co-operation our men had
received in Egypt and the treatment our scholars had enjoyed
in other foreign lands. I told them about a young scientist from
Michigan who had been living for some time in the then forbidden country of Tibet. I added that on my last expedition
to the tropics we had worked in a region where a party from
another institution had been chased out by the natives the year
before. As they listened politely, I gave them the crowning
touch by telling them that I was a member of a society composed of just three members, a German, an American professor,

and myself. We had the distinction of being the only people privileged to sit around a campfire of wild Carib Indians, drinking native beer from a gourd passed from hand to hand. (I did not tell them that I was so interested in listening to the Indians that I could drink the beer while watching the squaws sitting to one side chewing corn and throwing it into another pot to ferment for more beer.) Finally, one of the wise old Arabs said, "Dr. Ruthven, you probably can't understand because you are not an oriental. We reflect more than you do. It is our observation that the Michigan scholars we have seen have one common characteristic,—simple intellectual honesty." I have always hoped that this trait characterized the scholars who have represented us in foreign lands.

While in Cairo for the audience I left Mrs. Ruthven on the desert with the Arab servants. She has always said that she never had a more pleasant time or such interesting conversation. I don't know just how the conversation was conducted, but I do know that the natives could not speak English and she could not speak Arabic! Their sign language must have been wonderful.

Before we left Egypt we visited the royal tomb. In this beautiful structure with its elaborate furnishings at the period of Ramadan, there was in a case an illuminated copy of the Koran used by the king on ceremonial occasions. I knew that an "infidel" would profane a copy of the Koran by touching it, but being a booklover I instinctively put out my hand. The case was quickly closed. I started to apologize, when the lord chamberlain who was our guide, said to the caretaker, "Open the case and allow Dr. Ruthven to hold the book. He is not a Muslim, but he is a believer." Any booklover will understand what a pleasure it was for me to hold this magnificent work.

I thought Mrs. Ruthven might naturally be left out of things pertaining to these royal activities in view of the place women hold in Mohammedan society. She also shared, how-

ever, because she had from the Queen a gracious note express-
ing her regrets that because of Ramadan she could not receive
callers and giving her permission to visit the quarters to be occupied by the harem on the occasion of the services at the
tomb.

THE INSTRUCTORS

The instructors in my time, especially in the scientific
fields, formed a rather intimate group of young aspirants to
fame and fortune. Many of these friendships have continued
down through the years. We had great respect for our superiors,
but often felt we were better than they thought we were. We
agreed we were underpaid.

We had several theories, most of them wrong, on the factors deans and department chairmen used in recommending
promotions and salary increases. One allegedly judged his men
on the number of pages they had published, another on their
social activities. A third was supposed to support the view that
if the instructor was relatively affluent he was less entitled to a
raise than was a less privileged colleague. On occasion a careless
remark by an administrative officer seemed to confirm some of
our opinions.

I wanted to own an automobile. I could not afford the
luxury, but my brother-in-law was in the business and could get
one at cost. This was too great a temptation. For about $450
I became the proud owner of a shiny Model-T. As I was driving
down the street one day I passed the dean walking to campus
with an instructor, a close friend, who reported their conversation:

"Walter, wasn't that Ruthven in that automobile?"

"Yes, Dean E."

"Is it his?"

"I believe it is, Dean."

"Well, he certainly doesn't need a raise if he can afford a big car like that."

Anyone with aspirations to be somebody in the biological fields in which I was most interested realized that to succeed he had to consult the material in the British Museum of Natural History. This great storehouse of specimens and data, continuously being studied by some of the most distinguished scholars in the world, is both an inspiration and a necessary source of information.

I had two periods of study in it, with free access to the materials and to the advice and unpublished discoveries of the staff. Quite as important, I became acquainted with such scholars as Boulenger, Lord Rothschild, Bateson, and Parker, men with whom I subsequently worked closely through correspondence.

Outside of museum hours I had "bus-man's holidays" with these friends: a weekend with Bateson and his students, and visits with Lord Rothschild in his museum at Tring, Major Flower at his home, and Chalmers-Mitchell and Joan Proctor at the London Zoological Gardens. Two young scientists gave me an evening that only a young zoologist could fully appreciate.

The meeting was a session of the famous, old Linnaean Society. It was held in a small auditorium and was being opened by the presiding officer when we arrived. There were other places available, and I couldn't understand why my companions insisted that I sit in a particular rear seat. The speaker rose and stood behind a battered old desk. At that point a voice whispered to me: "Charles Darwin stood at that desk in this room when he read his first paper on the origin of species. You are sitting under his portrait." I felt as if I had been anointed.

Toward the end of my teaching career the governor of Michigan urged me strongly to accept an appointment as director of a state department giving him considerable difficulty. He took me up on a high mountain and showed me the scenery. The party had been in power for years. The leaders were in agreement on my appointment. If I would accept and hold the post for a period, I would advance to the legislature. From there I could choose one of two routes, to the governorship or to Congress. I was not tempted, but I had to have the help of the President of the University to remain free.

During these years I gave little classroom instruction. Early in the period I gave courses open to graduates and undergraduates in ecology, geographical distribution, conservation, and the history of zoology. I have been told that my course in conservation of wild life was the first one in the United States. When this course was first announced the students said they hoped it would live up to its title.

My principal, and later my exclusive, teaching responsibilities were with graduate students. These practically lived in the Museum. We did not even need organized seminars, for we felt free at all times to discuss the progress or lack of progress we were making in our researches. Instruction was a reciprocal effort and a very informal one.

My method was to discover the prospective student's field of interest, his sincerity, and ability, to advise him in the selection of his problem, and to help arrange a program of study best fitted to his needs. His grades as an undergraduate didn't interest me very much.

I fear in some cases we bent and even broke some University rules. The records of my students have not, however, caused me to regret such transgressions.

The young woman appeared quite unexpectedly in my office at the beginning of the semester. Students were supposed to enroll with me only with my permission. She had been admitted without prior consultation. Someone had erred. Since the fault was not hers—she was an out-of-state student and had been advised by a distinguished colleague in my field to work with me—I accepted her. After a few weeks both the lady and myself recognized that while an earnest student she was not the kind of clay that could be molded into a successful herpetologist. What was to be done? The time had elapsed during which she could have elected other work. For various reasons she needed an advanced degree. As I often did with my students I asked:

"What would you most like to be and do in this world?"

"I would like to be a photographer."

"A scientific artist I presume, not, heaven help us, a family picture-taker?"

"Neither, Dr. Ruthven, I should like to become a news photographer-reporter and a good one."

"Young lady, I believe you can do it, but we must be sure. Go up to the Museum studio and go to work. If and only if the director reports that you have exceptional ability I will at the end of the year recommend you for a master's degree in zoology. You understand this is quite illegal and must remain confidential until you achieve success or I retire."

The result? A distinguished foreign correspondent, author, and lecturer, a recipient of an honorary degree from the University, and a continuing inspiration to her "teacher."

THE MUSEUM STORY

Much of the history of the University Museum is recorded in the *Proceedings* of the Board of Regents, in the annual reports which Adams and I published, and in the Michigan *Encyclopedic Survey*. Among many stories of the early days I especially liked one concerning a well-known professor of forestry who became a personal friend in my first days as a curator.

He began his career at Michigan as an assistant in the Museum. For some reason it was decided to mount a bear for the exhibits and to give him the job. He was not a taxidermist. The results were not happy. The bear was lumpy in all the wrong places. Finally, after working for days on the project he became irritated and kicked the result of his labors down four flights of stairs. When the curator went to assess the damage he found a very good-looking stuffed bear. It was put in a case, where it remained for many years.

When Adams came to the University the Museum had for years been suffering from neglect. The study collections were unimportant and the exhibits unattractive. The building also housed the Department of Geology, a mineral collection, a large collection of musical instruments, and a Chinese exhibit presented to President Angell by the Chinese government. It was truly a hodgepodge.

The Museum was the butt of many campus jokes. Visitors seldom came to the building more than once, except for a few mothers who found it a convenient place to park their offspring. The storage specimens were only occasionally borrowed for class demonstrations. One of the more consistent users of the materials was a campus fraternity. As a part of their rites an initiate was required to steal a toenail of a mounted walrus. The toenails of our two mounted specimens never gave out, for after the initiations the taxidermist made new ones from goose quills.

The curator of the Museum had general charge of the building and the exhibits. Neither Adams nor I gave the latter much attention. The building was crowded, and we were too busy with our students and our studies and in augmenting the research collections. In short, our principal objective was to build a teaching and research unit.

The development of the Museum of Zoology was a slow and

sometimes painful business. The public had to learn that a curator did not pickle or stuff animals, that a museum was not a repository of freaks and curios, and that a specimen without data was all but useless. I had to refuse, as tactfully as possible, a two-headed calf, Aunt Mary's hair wreath, and grandfather's hunting trophies.

When it became known that I was a herpetologist I was frequently questioned about snakes. More old wives' tales have been told about these animals than about any other group. My opinion was often asked about the hoary old legend that snakes swallow their young for protection. This ridiculous superstition is hardy.

On one occasion I became irritated with a persistent reporter. "The man who says he saw young snakes run down their mother's gullet is either blind, a liar, or his snakes came from a bottle." The interview was published. A few days later I looked up from my desk to find a very large man in a dogskin coat leaning over me. He had blood in his eye. "Young man, do you mean to say my grandfather was a liar?" I wriggled out of this situation as best I could.

An appreciation of the Museum as a research and teaching unit grew slowly, but grow it did. The Museum was separated administratively from the Department of Zoology, and the budget and staff were enlarged. Graduate courses under the curators were added to the curriculum and field work was developed. The collections in other fields and the Department of Geology were removed from the building. Most importantly, the department gained international recognition as a teaching and research institution.

My concept of the place and functions of a museum in a university may be simply stated: It should be administered as an independent unit, ranking with the schools and colleges, not as an adjunct to a teaching unit.

The principal field of research in a museum of zoology should be systematic zoology in the broad and modern meaning of the term. This discipline involves more than the description of new species, nomenclatural squabbles, and geographic lists. It requires bringing to comparative morphology the facts of ecology, variation, geography, and geology in an attempt to throw light on the origin and history of animal forms and groups.

The study collections should be carefully prepared and filed and the specimens accompanied by detailed data. They should in effect constitute a library of specimens instead of books and not be a mere conglomeration of pickled and dried cadavers. The exhibits should illustrate biological principles, not awe the visitor with the skill of the taxidermist.

Even after we acquired full occupancy of the building and certain exhibits were dismantled to provide office and laboratory space, it was evident that if the museum was to grow and to achieve its avowed objectives a new building would have to be provided. This need was presented to the legislators several times. Finally, in the administration of Acting-President Lloyd, a museum building was given top priority among the capital needs of the University. The request was acted on favorably by the legislature.

Even before the funds became available the Regents had given me entire responsibility for the plan and design of the structure. I was able in the new building to separate, to the advantage of both, the exhibits and the research collections and laboratories.

Shortly after the legislature acted on the Museum bill I learned by the grapevine that the governor intended to veto the appropriation. The culmination of twenty-five years of planning was about to be scuttled. I called two of the Regents, who immediately went to Lansing, called on the governor, and expressed satisfaction with the action of the legislature. When he told them that he was about to veto the measure one of the

Regents picked up a pen, dipped it in ink, and leaned over the desk. "Governor, you are going to sign this bill and sign it now or I will throw this pen in your eye. I am taking the pen to Dr. Ruthven." His excellency signed on the dotted line.

Stimulus and Response—
Presidential Years

*It is not only paying wages, and giving
commands that constitute a master
of a family; but prudence, equal behavior,
with a readiness to protect and cherish
them, is what entitles man to that
character in their very hearts and
sentiments.*

INAUGURATION

MY FIFTH REBIRTH came one beautiful bright sunny morning as I was sitting on a pile of lumber watching and, I hoped, supervising the materialization of a dream—the construction of a new building for a museum of natural history. As I was thinking over certain last problems of the building, my friend Dr. C. C. Little, then President of the University, came across the street. He greeted me with the announcement that I was to be dean of administration of the University. The position corresponded to a vice-presidency.

This was a distinct shock. I refused to consider the appointment, for my life was organized and my goals set, but he convinced me that he was in trouble in his administration, particularly as far as the deans were concerned, and they had agreed on my appointment. We finally arrived at a compromise. I could continue my studies and retain my positions as director of the Museum and chairman of the Department of Zoology and give him the assistance he needed for one year. Little did I know what was to happen within the period!

Toward the close of the year the President resigned. The Regents requested me to continue my responsibilities as dean of administration through the summer, during which time they promised to fill both posts. To my great discomfiture, their deliberations continued into the fall.

My experiences as dean during this trying period later proved invaluable. I became well acquainted with the deans and their problems. Having charge of the budget I gained a knowledge of faculty and departmental difficulties. Most important, perhaps, I had to determine without delay what would be the best policies and methods in dealing with the legislature. In short, I had to learn to swim or sink. For the University it was a time of confusion.

SOME GENERAL PROBLEMS

When I was drawing up my first budget as dean of administration I was warned not to use the term "tuition." I learned that by Act no. 151 of 1851, the legislature provided in section 13 as follows: "The University shall be open to all persons resident of this state, without charge of tuition, under the regulations prescribed by the Regents; and to all other persons under such regulations and restrictions as the Board may prescribe."

This legislation, the Regents informed me, was clearly unconstitutional and had been ignored. Curiously, however, the attorney general in 1901 saw fit to deliver the following opinion: "The Board of Regents of the University of Michigan has power to determine fees to be paid by citizens of this state and other states and is not subject to legislative control in this matter."

It is interesting to note that early in the history of the University there were evidently objections to tuition charges for resident students. Also to my nonlegal mind the opinion of the attorney general was a subterfuge resorted to because the University, fifty years later, did not care to revive the issue on which the legislature had taken action.

I have contended for years that public-supported institutions of higher learning should not charge more than nominal tuition (or fees) to instate students. It does not make good sense to insist that we need more college-trained citizens and at the same time to cut down the supply at the high-school level by increasing costs of further training to the student or his family. I have never found sympathetic ears for this contention outside of Russia.

The summer after Dr. Little's retirement was particularly unpleasant for me and my family. The reporters were having a Roman holiday by digging up, inventing, or playing up rumors, gossip, interviews, and comments. The situation was confusing to the public and embarrassing to everyone who was or might be or should not be considered for the position of president. The University atmosphere was charged with doubt and uncertainty, as is customary during interregna in academic institutions.

Prior to a regular monthly meeting in the fall, the Board of Regents was in conference on the situation. As dean of administration and acting chief executive, I was in my office awaiting a call for the agenda. The call came; I entered the board room and approached the desk of the presiding officer. To my surprise it was occupied by a Regent who gave no indication of yielding the chair. It was an embarrassing moment, made the more so by the solemn faces of the members of the Board. I stood in uncertainty with no place to go. I then heard a motion to place the presidential mantle on my shoulders. It was duly seconded and passed. I was in a daze, having never even been approached on the matter. Realizing that I should make some acknowledgment I tried to get my ideas together. As I was stammering some sort of acknowledgment one of the members exclaimed in vigorous tones and with a friendly smile, "Oh, hell, Mr. President, sit down. We shoved the chair under you and we can jerk it out again." The tension was broken with hearty laughter. Then my acceptance speech came to me. "You will never get a chance to let me down that way, Mr. Regent. When you reach for the chair I will not be in it." This was the only inauguration I would permit.

I have often been asked by scientist friends why I sacrificed a career in science—for which I had made careful preparation— for an administrative position. My studies were progressing satisfactorily. I had a dedicated and able young staff and a promising group of graduate students. The Museum had acquired valued patrons and was gaining international recognition. I do not think personal ambition was much of a factor. The University was badly disorganized, and I knew the problems, at least some of the answers, and felt obligated to the institution to which I owed so much.

The Regents never divulged to me their reasons for my appointment. I prefer not to believe the students were right in concluding the selection was made on the assumption that a herpetologist could handle the faculty!

The family name has not been easy to live with in the United States. With strangers it usually has to be spelled. No matter how carefully enunciated it is more than likely to be understood as "Ruthben," "Ruthaven," "Rutheven," or even "Rutherford."

Shortly after taking on my new responsibilities my secretary informed me that the office people across the campus would like to know how to pronounce my name. I explained that in olden days in Scotland it was pronounced "Riven" with the R strongly burred. Later, both in England and Scotland it became Rŭthven with a short *u*. Finally, in the United States it was usually Rūthven with a long *u* to those with other than a British background. I added facetiously, "You secretaries can decide the question." Their decision was for Rūthven to the disapproval of the family and my British colleagues.

After my appointment came a period of twenty-two years as President of the University. The time included a great depression, bank closings, a world war, and other crises.

Mrs. Ruthven and I decided at once that much as we regretted leaving the new house we had built it would be in the best interests of the University if we moved into the President's home on the campus. There seem to be two schools of thought among college presidents in respect to their residences. According to one the President should live close to his work; the other thinks it better for him to be far enough away so that he is not readily available in the small crises that occur almost daily on a large campus.

There are a few important compensations for living on the campus. For the student with a problem for which, at least in his opinion, he can get a solution from no one else, the opportunity to talk with the President often means much to his future. The staff member who knows he can go to the President with a personal problem outside of office hours gains the feeling of being a part of a human institution rather than a mere employee. The parent concerned about the welfare of a son or a daughter feels closer to the institution if he can in emergencies call the President himself.

Knowing that we would be living in a goldfish bowl we nevertheless did not hesitate to move to the campus, install three telephones in the house, and proceed to let parents, staff members, students, and alumni know that they were welcome to appeal for help at any hour of the day or night.

Naturally, there were disadvantages in this ready accessibility, but the University telephone operators soon eliminated certain ones. They became proficient in recognizing the voices of celebrating alumni who insisted on calling the President at four in the morning to inquire about his health, and in tracing the calls of such mentally disturbed persons as the woman who each year asked Mrs. Ruthven on Commencement Day to stop driving white horses past her home.

The furnishings for the house were our responsibility, and we decided that they should reflect the type of architecture and the Angell tradition. Being a family of collectors we had through the years assembled pictures and other art objects and interesting and rare books which we arranged to attract student attention. We also placed in the library copies of the publications of members of the faculty and a bronze bas-relief of President Angell. Our objective was to create an interesting home atmosphere for the family, the staff, the alumni, and particularly the students.

We made it a practice to entertain University guests in our home whenever possible. This we considered was both a courtesy to our visitors and a privilege for the family. During the years we had many intimate visits with writers, scientists, actors, college presidents, legislators, and governors, among others. These visits were always pleasant, usually informative, often exciting, and occasionally amusing.

An old friend, a distinguished poet, and a lovable man discovered after dinner and just before his public reading that he had forgotten copies of the poems he proposed to recite. Did I have a copy of his collected works? I did. "To repay you for the use of this book I will read first the poem of your selection." Naturally, I chose "The Morgan Colt." In announcing the poem he remarked to the audience that it was a favorite of mine, and he was reading from the Morgan Horse Edition of his poems. As the audience was leaving the hall after the talk, I was stopped by two instructors in English. They told me they had thought they knew all of the editions of Frost's poems, but had never heard of the Morgan Horse Edition. I could only tell them that I was not surprised for only one copy had ever been printed and I had it. I have often wondered for how many years this bit of misinformation was passed along to students.

There was anticipation and consternation in the family. The First Lady of the land was to be a guest for a day or two. In the campus "White House," celebrities were an old story and were usually taken in stride. Its roof had sheltered, without noticeable strain, foreign diplomats, members of royal families, lords and ladies, governors, legislators, distinguished scholars, noted artists, and actors good and bad. But here was a disturbing complication. The lady would find upon arrival a damsel with whom she would have to compete for the affections of her hosts and the students—a real college widow.

The distinguished guest had a pleasing personality, an attractive albeit not beautiful face, and an interest in youth. She did not like the Dies Committee. She was the wife of a President, but did not suffer from it.

Her rival was also not beautiful by accepted standards. Her teeth were exposed, and her legs were conspicuously bowed. She loved students, and the only person she had ever bitten was a Republican. She was the girl friend of a President.

Both were named "Eleanor."

What to do? The students were agog, the family nervous. Would the guest object to having an English bulldog as a namesake? Could the family get through the visit without using the name? Evidently, anyone calling "Eleanor" might create an embarrassing situation.

By exercising great vigilance, lying to newshawks, threatening the maids, and bribing the children, the secret was kept.

The two ladies became fast friends, no embarrassing questions were asked, honor was preserved, and the family escutcheon was kept unstained.

There were mutual congratulations as the visitor was speeded on her way. But an epilogue to the tale partakes of the nature of a prologue.

In due time another visitor appeared who promptly asked: "How did you like my friend—Madam, the wife of the President?"

"Oh, very much," I replied, "we never had a more delightful guest."

Exclaimed the visitor, "I am so glad! Before she came to the campus, she remarked that she wanted to meet the Ruthvens. She thought they must approve of her to have given her name to their very favorite pet."

I have been told by her friends that I was the first to introduce this grand woman to an audience as "the former first lady of the United States—now the first lady of the world."

A well-known actress and writer after an evening performance enjoyed refreshments and conversation with friends. On such an occasion, discussing various subjects, one of the group mentioned my horses. For the rest of the evening the lady regaled us with a hilarious account of her experiences as a wife and mother, who allegedly did not like horses, in a family of horse-lovers. Months afterward we received her book. Evidently she had used us as guinea pigs. We must have convinced Miss Skinner that her book would be a success.

We always told our guests they could say anything they wanted to say in our home and deny it afterward if they should hear themselves quoted to their embarrassment. They generally seemed to accept this statement at its face value. At any rate we were privileged on many an occasion to hear and take part in frank discussions, on delicate or controversial subjects, by diplomats, lawmakers, laborites, industrialists, and scholars in many fields. These confidences were never violated even by students when present. We took it as a compliment when a friend remarked, "Mr. President, your home is a real 'confessional.' "

Of course, we lived in a "goldfish bowl." Fortunately, we were able to keep some experiences from the press that would have made good reading. One of these was the discovery that a trusted houseman had stolen a telephone instrument, cleverly tapped a wire, and been for an unknown length of time an agent in the numbers racket.

ADMINISTRATION

Immediately on assuming the duties of President I found I had to learn many things about university administration both fast and often the hard way—by study, trial, and error. Some of the observations I record may appear to grizzled occupants of presidential chairs as expositions of the obvious. They nevertheless set forth some things a new president had to discover for himself.

Not unlikely, in the opinion of some, my vision was at times myopic and my thinking naive. I shall not attempt to reply to such criticisms. After all, it is my life and these are my recollections and reflections. Let others perform the autopsy.

Owing to the circumstances, the University was disorganized. The deans had necessarily become quite autocratic. On many occasions they went directly to the Regents, bypassing the President with their suggestions and problems. I thought that a university at its best is more than the sum of its parts. It should be more than a mere assemblage of schools and colleges; it should have emergent values from integration. This unity is not easy for a chief administrator to obtain and maintain, for students, staff members, including deans, and alumni are properly accustomed to thinking for themselves. Again, trustees, like members of schoolboards generally, tend to think of themselves as educators, which they generally are not, and to forget that their function is a corporate and not an administrative one.

The role of mediator in family misunderstandings is a dangerous one. He may cause a temporary suspension of a family row, but it is quite as likely that both participants will attack him. A college president should then probably not be surprised to find himself rather continuously in hot water. He stands, or should stand, squarely between the staff and the trustees and between the deans of the different schools and colleges. With the best of intentions these groups often experience difficulty in understanding each other's problems.

Trustees are prone to think of faculty members as impractical and visionary, to view instruction as too theoretical, and even to be somewhat doubtful of the business sense of administrative officers at all levels. Faculty members often look upon trustees as hard-boiled, narrow-minded business or professional people, would-be dictators or self-appointed Pharisees, who do not understand that education moves forward and youth is not being prepared for the world of today but for the world of tomorrow.

Members of governing boards often seem to be sensitive souls who, like many so-called "practical" persons, lose their sense of proportion when they find themselves in posts of distinction which touch areas outside their own fields of competence. They are likely to consider their election or appointment as a sort of laying-on of hands by virtue of which they have suddenly become educators. Professors are likewise sensitive and serious about their profession, jealous of their prerogatives, proud of their achievements, and as resentful of unintelligent criticism and interference with their work as any other group of experts.

One of the major tasks of a president who would build an

integrated institution is to keep peace in the family by harmonizing, not compromising, the different viewpoints. Simultaneously, he must train his trustees to have confidence in their faculties and instruct the faculty in the problems of a governing board.

I came to believe that university administrators are worth their salt to the degree to which they delegate authority *without shirking responsibility*. This principle applies to boards in control as well as to presidents, deans, business managers, and other college officers. When a trustee endeavors to decide such matters as the selection of academic personnel, the admission of students, the awarding of degrees (honorary or earned), and the drafting of curricula, he becomes an actual, or at least a potential, liability to the institution. He may have been an athlete in his day, but this does not qualify him to hire or fire a coach. If he is or has been a distinguished member of a profession the chances are that he knows little about present-day programs and trends in professional training. If he is a business man, he may not fully appreciate the importance of a liberal education and tend to be impatient with the slow, laborious nature of the creative activities of staff members. It is particularly difficult for some trustees to realize that the colleges are continually changing and that these institutions are more complex than they appear to the former student or to others outside of their walls.

Staff members for their part do not always realize that their work is not the only important activity in the college—that in fact their departments owe their very existence to the organization of which they are a part. The chiefs should not use the governing board as an ogre to frighten younger staff members or attempt to take advantage of colleagues by going to members of the board in control with their problems.

Obvious as it would seem, it is often overlooked in college administration that the proper function of governing boards is to work with faculties and administrative officers for a co-ordinated institution. The board has the responsibility of keeping the college solvent, of seeing that support of the several activities is properly proportioned, of evaluating the services of the executive officers in the light of the objectives of the organization, and of protecting the faculties in their attempts to push society along the road to a better world order.

Admittedly, the president is liable to be blown out of the water at any time if he tries to be both mediator and teacher. This is a risk he should take gladly, for his dual role is an all-important one. If he is conscientious he may expect to succeed more easily with the faculty, for he can see them every day, whereas he meets his board only at intervals. The best he can do is to be patient and tireless. The first Board of Regents with which I served gave each new member this advice: "Keep still and listen for a year."

My first task was rather easily accomplished. I was able to convince the deans that we could work together only if they took problems that required regental action to the Board through me or at least with my knowledge. They also agreed to draw their faculties into the administration of their units by forming executive committees.

A short time after taking office I became appalled at the number of activities, large and small, over which I had direct supervision. Besides the schools and colleges, some eighteen departments, boards, and committees reported directly to the President and on several he was ex-officio chairman. It was not difficult to demonstrate to the Regents that a different type of organization was needed. They approved of a plan to spread executive duties.

The committees of the Board of Regents were eliminated. Vice-presidents and directors were given specific supervisory responsibilities under the President. I resigned from most boards and committees. The President's staff formed a "cabinet" which met at my home regularly once each week, more often when necessary. The members of this group also met with the conference of deans and were present at meetings of the Board of Regents.

The faculties and deans at first had some reservations about the plan, fearing that it would interpose executives between them and the President, but their fears were soon dispelled. Problems were dealt with expeditiously. The Regents were given well-considered agendas. An appreciable amount of time was saved for deans, department heads, and the Regents.

While the Regents continued to meet each month, the sessions were shortened. I was never convinced that in a well-organized institution *regular* meetings of the directors needed to be held more frequently than quarterly.

Certainly, the new plan afforded me much relief. I no longer needed to make almost daily, quick decisions on such diverse matters as changes in the dental curriculum, the provision of a rest room for women in the Law School, additions to the faculty, and the dismissal of the son of a prominent alumnus, who seemed to be more interested in supporting the beer industry than in his grades. Finally, I had more time for individual conferences and planning.

Administration under the plan operated rather smoothly for about my first ten years in office, partly because the University had a Board of experienced Regents. Three new members, coming on the Board about that time, caused a crisis not easily weathered. It began when I informed the Board of my thinking that they should not interfere in matters properly the business of the staff, but concern themselves exclusively with their corporate responsibilities. With few exceptions, the staff stood with me on this principle of administration.

The three new regents formed a (nonpolitical) coalition. They insisted they had a right to interview the members of the staff on their problems, to have certain privileges, such as the admission of unqualified students, to determine where purchases should be made (sometimes in favor of their clients), and to take the initiative if they chose to do so in the promotion, hiring, and dismissal of staff members. This battle was waged for a number of years, but thanks to the support of the administrative officers and a majority of one on the Board, the administration was never forced to yield in important cases.

The attitude of the three regents mentioned was aggravated by a statement of mine on the entry of the United States in World War II, when I addressed the students on their responsibilities. Briefly, I said that I regretted that their work would be interfered with by world conditions which had come about through no fault of theirs but were the result of the stupidity of their elders. I knew, however, that they would accept their responsibilities and do their part in trying to bring about a better future. Speaking as I was to college students, I considered it more honest to explain the business frankly than to try to arouse emotions by beating the drums and waving the flag.

Later, I also opposed the first plans of the armed forces to take over large parts of the institution and to put in their own training programs. The University, I insisted, was best able to carry on several specific training programs that would be needed as the conflict progressed, and certain types of training which could be given only by the armed services should be conducted in other than educational institutions. Fortunately, again I had the staff with me, and it was with satisfaction that, at the close of the war, I received for the University high praise from the military command for our stand and for the quality of our training programs.

The three regents referred to objected to my talk to the students and to my attitude on the supervision of administrative functions. For several months they carried a copy of what was to be my resignation to the meetings hoping to persuade a majority of the Board to ask for it. This they were unable to do, I believe, because the staff and the experienced Board members approved of my thoughts on organization and knew that I assumed full responsibility for any stand I felt required to take. I tried never to forget the admonition of former President Harry B. Hutchins: "Remember the University pays you to make the disagreeable as well as the pleasant decisions."

A confusing practice of the Board at this time was the habit of the minority group of caucusing before each meeting. This was apparently something new in the history of the University and, of course, contrary to the best interests of the institution.

In another schism in the Board, I found myself allied with a minority group for a time. After World War I, sites for veterans' hospitals had been determined largely by political pressures. The results were far from satisfactory. On recommendations of doctors themselves after World War II, the Veterans Administration wisely erected new hospitals near medical schools to secure the advantages of their facilities and services.

When it was decided to place a hospital in Ann Arbor and integrate its services with those of the Medical School there was opposition on the Board. The arguments were shopworn: "More veterans' hospitals aren't needed." "There are enough doctors to care for the veterans." "These hospitals will soon be caring for nonservice as well as service-connected cases." "It's a step toward socialized medicine." The arguments went on for months. Finally, under the leadership of two regents and with the full support of the faculty of the Medical School differences were resolved. Even before the building was completed a plan of cooperation had been adopted, which has proven very successful.

Pressures on state universities by members of the legislature have sometimes been the result of opposition from special interests. Not even the constitutional status of the University of Michigan has left it free from such pressures. Once in my experience the Regents yielded to such an attack.

The University had enthusiastically organized adult educa-

tion courses for workers, similar to those long conducted successfully in Great Britain. The labor unions had been convinced that
these courses were educational in the best sense. Everything went
well until an instructor gave as assigned reading a union pamphlet on a struggle then going on between one of the most
powerful companies in the United States and a labor union. In
this contest the company strenuously criticized the wage demands of labor, the president loudly insisting, of course, that
the company could not afford the increases. The union claimed
that the company operations were extremely profitable, that the
salary of the president was several hundred thousand dollars a
year, and that he could not be very much worried about his own
living expenses since he had just purchased a prize bull at a cost
of thousands of dollars.

I never knew whether the president of the company thought
that the pamphlet insulted him or the bull. He became extremely angry and would listen to no explanations. With the
prestige of his company to support him, he brought pressures to
bear on regents through state legislators and Michigan representatives in Congress. This happened when the University had the
divided Board, and for the first time in the history of the institution, to my knowledge, it yielded to the pressures. The director
of the program was discharged and the courses abolished.

I did not feel too bad about the fate of the program, for
since its inception, several universities had adopted similar projects, the unions had expanded their educational activities, and
the experience of Michigan would certainly demonstrate to other
institutions the probabilities of political interference with courses
in worker education in any way critical of management. " 'Tis
true, 'tis pity; and pity 'tis 'tis true."

This is an appropriate place to acknowledge my indebtedness to Shirley W. Smith. As secretary and later as vice-president
and secretary he was business manager of the University from
the James B. Angell era through most of my regime. He was an

able executive and a dedicated University official. He gave me much valuable advice and never failed to co-operate with me even when he thought I was inclined to treat some old traditions with scant courtesy.

Being a man of integrity and at the same time a sensitive soul, Shirley suffered keenly during the period of our trouble with the Regents. He was criticized and even threatened with dismissal for his steadfast refusal to approve purchases of supplies of inferior quality or at exorbitant costs. At one time the situation became so serious that he initiated the following correspondence:

March 11, 1942

Dear Alex:

Herewith I am handing you a communication which I know you will treat as confidential, between ourselves only, until you shall believe that in accordance with its terms, action should be taken on it, whether today or whenever. Please accept it at face value.

While I shall be happy to stay on in my place as long as it is felt I am needed, and to continue relations with you that have given me increasingly not only happiness in my time but an increasingly deep affection for you, you could do me no greater disservice than to let me outstay my usefulness.

Use your *judgment*, not your kindness of heart only.

As always,
Shirley

March 11, 1942

President Alexander G. Ruthven,
    Angell Hall
Dear Dr. Ruthven:

Observation over a long period has convinced me that men often do not recognize a lowering of their efficiency and of the value of their service as they grow older. I have for a long time been determined that I would not put or leave myself in a position that might involve embarrassment or expense to the University that I love by any sort of unearned consideration for me. Therefore I desire this communication to be regarded by you as my resignation as Vice President and Secretary of the University, to be presented by you to the Regents and accepted by them at any time, now or later, when it is your considered opinion that a younger man in my present position would be likely to give services more valuable to the University than my own. I would assume that acceptance would be subject to my admission to the usual retiring allowance.

Sincerely yours,
Shirley W. Smith

Dear Shirley:

As you have asked I will be very frank. If the times were normal I would be inclined to accept your resignation for the sole reason that one who has carried the heavy load you have should in his later years have time to have a respite. As it is I feel both you and I can serve our country best at this time by doing the things we can do best. You should, and I am sure you want to, stay by this ship. When the storm subsides perhaps we can both with better grace give the helm to some younger officers. The members of our Tuesday group all have different temperaments. This is natural and it makes life and work interesting. Fortunately we can work together, and I hope we can continue as a group, at least until better times.

I need not tell you, Shirley, how much I have enjoyed our association. We have disagreed on some things, which is just as it should be if people are good friends as well as business associates. On some of these occasions I have been convinced that I was right. On others you have been right and by yielding to your judgment I have avoided serious difficulties. This again is just as it should be.

Let us stick together on this job for a while longer and do what we can to keep the old boat on an even keel.

Yours most sincerely,

March 16, 1942   Alex

As "watchdog of the treasury" Shirley Smith sometimes disappointed members of the staff, but all in all the University never had a more faithful servant.

The selection of candidates for honorary degrees was always a time-consuming and arduous task. It was a faculty responsibility. Nominations were made to the Board of Regents by a Senate committee. This committee in my time solicited proposals from each member of the academic staff.

The requests for names to be processed by the committee were usually made before the Christmas recess. The proposals were to be fully documented. The suggestions were studied by the committee both by the individual members and in conference. Nominations were then made to the Board of Regents.

The eligibility standards were rigid and jealously guarded. Scholarship or public service were prerequisites to consideration of the proposed candidates. I often referred to the committee as the eye of the needle at this entrance to the University. Generous donors were usually suspect. Only the intellectually elite and humanitarians in the best sense of the term had a chance of being admitted.

The functions of the Board of Regents in this matter were seen by the committee and by the members of the Board, except for a short period, to be to determine the number of degrees to be awarded each year and to reject nominations which, on the basis of information not available to the committee, would not reflect credit on the University. About midway in my term of office a few of the Regents proposed to add names to the list of recipients on their own responsibility. I insisted that they should either submit their proposals to the Senate committee for approval or refuse to recognize the committee. Since the majority of the Board had no desire to submit themselves to the inevitable pressures from alumni, friends, business associates, and politicians, the controversy was settled without a serious rift.

With the retirement of two regents who constituted what I have called the minority group and their replacements with two new members there was a change in the attitude of the Board. During the final years I was in office it again demonstrated in its actions the singleness of purpose, wisdom, and ability which has guided the University during most of its history. The return to the Michigan tradition of a co-operative governing body familiar with the history and ideals of the institution was greatly facilitated by the quiet and respected leadership of a new member. He was a man of scholarly interests, familar with the history of the University and appreciative of the true meaning of higher education. In addition, he was adept in reading my mind. Often when I was having difficulty in presenting a proposal to the Board he would seize the ball and carry it over the goal.

An interim appointment to the Board of Regents was to be made by the governor of the state. For some time the alumnae had been agitating for the appointment of a woman to the Board. His excellency was irritated by the tactics of an energetic committee which had selected and publicly announced its candidate without consulting him. I was in his office on University business when his secretary entered with a message. A high-school friend of his was in town for a very short time and was anxious to pay her respects. I offered to withdraw, but the governor insisted I meet the lady. After a brief visit, he suggested that I take the caller to lunch and he would join us shortly.

Afterward, we were to meet again and take up University matters.

It was a most pleasant luncheon and the beginning of a long friendship. At its close we bade the lady good-bye and returned to the office, only to be told that the alumnae committee was waiting in the reception room. On receiving the message, the governor pondered the situation and turned to me.

"Dr. Ruthven, I have an idea."

"Governor, I know what it is. When did it come to you?"

"Just now. How did you like Esther?"

"Your Excellency, I do not concern myself with the appointment or election of regents, but if you have decided on Esther as our first woman Board member, I heartily approve of your decision."

The regents were somewhat apprehensive of having a woman on the Board. Their expressed fear was that with the best of intentions she would be a champion of the interests of her sex and of little assistance in dealing with broad University problems. Their fears were groundless. The new regent dispelled them at her first meeting when she announced: "Gentlemen, I expect to be a woman regent, not a women's regent."

Among the traits which faculty members share with many other people—and this to the distress of college presidents—is suspicion of authority. With few exceptions they are willing to accept administrative positions but as soon as one of them "crosses the line" he is set apart. Do the best he can, when he becomes a dean, department head, or president, his colleagues place their friendships with him on a different basis. He often feels as if he had suddenly become the carrier of a mild infection or at least has had a change in personality. I experienced this to some degree to my disappointment.

For years I had been a member of a small group of distinguished scholars who met once a month to exchange ideas. I had developed a warm feeling of personal friendship for these men. At the first meeting after my appointment one of them who had been asked to speak for the others told me that they would always be friends, but I must remember I was now in a different position. I could not expect the same intimacy that had characterized our relationships up to that time. It was a shock to me.

The selection of administrators is one of the toughest jobs which fall to the lot of a college president. The staff always has an abundance of good fellows, personal friends, excellent teachers, and outstanding researchers to whom a chief executive would gladly, if he could with safety, give anything loose around the place. Success in other fields does not, however, indicate ability in administration. It is not safe to take the course suggested by a disgruntled professor—select executives from among those who know too little to teach and conduct research. Again, the task of selecting officials cannot safely be delegated to trustees because they are not usually sufficiently informed as to the educational problems and trends in the several disciplines. Finally, it is seldom satisfactory to permit faculties to select their own leaders by committee action. Professors are naturally anxious to forward their own work and are great respecters of senatorial courtesy. A ballot to select a leader is almost sure to result in a compromise nominee.

The qualifications of an administrator are naturally the same in a college as in any other organization. They include knowledge of objectives and needs of the units, ability to work with others, some facility in organization, willingness to devote the necessary time to the routine duties of the position and to becoming acquainted with the conditions in the whole field of activity represented by a complex institution. One other qualification which should not be overlooked is an appreciation of the proper relationships which should exist between the several units. Deans and department heads may otherwise be excellent executives and still be failures through inability to become "university minded."

In my early years as president I endeavored to learn from presidents of other universities the most successful way of choosing executives. I was shocked to find that some of them felt that faculty members should have no part in choosing their leaders. I could not subscribe to this view. As a teacher I had sympathized with the feeling of my associates that they should have some part in the process.

I also discovered presidents who, whenever possible, took the easy way of bringing in men from other institutions because they did not have the courage to choose between two or more of their own men. This was justified by the excuse that the school should avoid "inbreeding." This is a ridiculous misuse of a term with specific meaning in biology but with no logical significance in staff appointments in a university. I have on many occasions seen good men passed by in favor of "outsiders" when executive posts were to be filled only to have these men eagerly snapped up by some other institution. Surely a university should be concerned with training its own administrators and should find it profitable to do so.

I finally worked out a method which I believe operated rather successfully for administrative posts. After having had some experience with faculty committees who recommended men who were clearly compromises, I assumed full responsibility for appointments which I made after personal and confidential conferences with the more experienced men in the units concerned. The appointments took cognizance of the abilities of the members of the staff and also of faculty evaluations of men in our own and other institutions who might be considered. In this plan the responsibility of the president is clear-cut, simple, and demanding. He must get all of the information he can about every possible candidate within and outside of the university, sell his final judgment to the trustees, and then pray that he hasn't made a serious mistake.

In this connection I want to brand as false the good-natured quip heard on the campus after two surprise appointments: "If a member of the staff has a horse he has a good chance of becoming a dean."

It early became evident to me that a large university is in one respect like an ant colony. One can seldom be sure of finding any given worker at any given time. My harassed secretary's favorite reply to my request to call a staff member was: "If I can't reach him on the campus, I will call the railroad stations and airport. He will be sure to be going or coming."

As instructor, dean, and president, I approved of most peregrinations of staff members. In fact I encouraged the deans to include fair allowances for travel in their budgets. Soon after becoming dean of administration, however, I discovered that the deans themselves were not always aware of the whereabouts of their staff members. The climax came when we needed to consult one of the department heads and found that he had departed on a three-months' trip without prior notice. The deans agreed that thereafter all absences should be approved by them and the longer ones reported in advance to the President's office. The regulations seemed reasonable enough, but they became effective very slowly.

On one occasion I endeavored to help a dean by calling the attention of his faculty to the matter in a lightly sarcastic paper read at a conference. At his request it is here recorded.

Ladies and Gentlemen:

My official duty and privilege on this occasion is to welcome you to the campus of the University. This I do most sincerely, although, of course, you do not need to be told that we are glad to have you with us. Your colleagues on our staff wanted you to come to our town, and the administrative officers figured it would cost less to have you here than to pay the expenses of half of the faculty to some far distant place.

Having said this, I am inclined to sit down and call it a day. But, alas, I am supposed to make a speech; I am expected, as a University president, to say something deans and professors can criticize. Under these circumstances, I have decided that the best I can do for you and myself is to refrain from ringing the changes on an unnecessary welcome, and break a tradition among official glad-handers by reading a scientific paper. If this is letting down the staff of our school, so be it. They have on plenty of occasions failed to spare my feelings.

I propose, then, without asking your permission, to summarize the results of a research upon which I have been engaged for some time. There is nothing improper in this decision, for underneath the robe and frozen visage which make a college president is, in my case, the lean, hard-bitten soul of a scientist, interested in the truth, the whole truth, and nothing but the truth.

The investigation I shall review for you has been entitled: "The survival of a primitive instinct, or the periodic migrations of professors." It was prompted by the observation of a harassed university president that he could never be quite sure of finding any given member of the staff on the job at any given time. As a corollary to this observation, it was discovered that the explanations given by well-trained secretaries, while usually very plausible, are extremely variable and sometimes even cleverly deceptive. The essential question posed for the investigator may then be phrased as follows: If a professor isn't here, why isn't he, and where is he?

No scientist could resist the temptation to take up such an interesting problem, and a study was begun, not so much to obtain immediately practical results as to discover the general principles, if any, involved in the temporary disappearance of staff members. In other words, it is research pure and undefiled rather than a clinical study. Note, I apply the word "pure" to the investigation, not to the professors. Our teachers are prone to insist that they are of the "pure in heart" who will some day see their Maker, although this has sometimes been disputed. But I leave this problem to others; I wouldn't know.

The methods used in the research were simple. Careful records were kept of absences from the campus over a ten-year period. The data assembled include names and ranks of absentees, alleged reasons for absences, and places to which pilgrimages were made. These were studied with the collaboration of our expert mathematicians, geographers, and meteorologists. Probable errors were computed, correlations worked out, and the distribution of the places visited was carefully charted on outline maps. Off the record, the material was also submitted to our religious experts, but, after a brief examination of the activities of professors when far from home, they commented, somewhat wistfully, that the phenomena were very far outside of their field. They offered but one suggestion: The elder statesmen, the grizzled veterans on the faculty, should be warned to remember on their trips that when new wine is poured into old bottles something usually happens. (This is a scriptural allusion.)

The results of my collaborators are believed to be accurate within the limits of the investigation and are herewith summarized.

1. The higher the rank of the teacher, the more frequent the absences. Assistant professors disappear more often than instructors, professors more frequently than assistant professors. As for the deans, they are mostly on the wing.
2. The more frequent the absences, the more periodic they are apt to be.
3. The periodic absences are definitely correlated with changes in the seasons.

4. The seasonal wanderings are closely associated with the meetings of societies and associations; the nonperiodic are in the
nature of sick leaves, visits to ailing grandmothers, personal
business, and other emergencies.

5. Finally, the regular wanderings of teachers, like the migrations of other birds, are usually from warm to cold latitudes
in the summer and from cold to warm regions in the winter.
The variations are associated with hunting and fishing seasons, football games, and other amusements which are seasonal in occurrence.

The conclusions would seem to be obvious. We have here
the survival of the instinct to migrate, common in animals,
particularly in our feathered friends. Professors and deans, like
other animal migrants, show a strong tendency to move toward
pleasant places. The phenomenon appears to develop with ad-
vancement in rank and therefore with age, although it is not
proper to say, as one of my assistants remarked in the course of
the study, that, apparently, the ranker the professor the more
he moves about.

Admittedly, the instinct may be better developed in the
younger men than is apparent. In other words, instructors and
assistant professors may have to resist an urge to fly the coop
because someone has to keep the student's *apex nasi* (or beak)
in his books. We can only make an inference here, but this
apparent failure in the data need not disturb us, for we only
started out to explain the absences as we find them, not the
suppressed desires of the staff.

Obviously, then, since instincts are, as we know, deeply
rooted in the protoplasm, our educators, with their meetings,
will probably continue to wander about, from Mackinac to New
Orleans, from Sun Valley to Atlantic City, from golf courses to
trout streams, and from football fields to duck marshes. They
are more to be pitied than censured. We must forgive them, for

they know not what they do. Presidents will have to be satisfied with understanding the nature of their wanderings and with trying to catch them between flights.

As evidence that this is a bona fide research I now point out that it may be carried farther, with profit at least to the investigator. If it is glandular disturbances which make the swallows come back to Capistrano, as some zoologists insist, it is possible that this is a factor in the peregrinations of professors. The possibility is strengthened by the fact that glands do change with age, and we now know from my researches that professor-migration is also a phenomenon which increases as years are accumulated. But here we need more evidence. Before experimenting with gland extracts, I submit we should know how the professors feel and act while on their journeys. On this point they are very reticent, or at least remarkably vague.

I am, therefore, according to the practice of investigators the world over, concluding this dissertation with a request. To continue my studies for another ten years, I respectfully petition any or all foundations for a grant of $25,000. It is coming on cold weather, and, if I can have the money in the near future, I will go south to do some deep sea fishing while awaiting the first visitors on their winter migration.

If I can get this help, I guarantee at least to see and study some of the members of my own staff—in New Orleans, in Florida, in Los Angeles, or, maybe, even in Tia Juana.

The rules put in force after this talk brought some order into problems of staff absences. I am sure, however, that as far as my office was concerned the regulations were at times honored in the breach rather than in the observance.

If one university activity more than any other is calculated to bring a president's gray hairs in sorrow to the grave it is inter-collegiate athletics. Intercollege athletic competitions inevitably become involved with educational standards, the hiring of athletes, and large capital investments for physical education. They arouse the emotions of the alumni, often to no good purpose. They attract a large public following interested only in the games as spectacles or as a source of profit and distort the true image of institutions of higher learning.

As dean of administration I had noted that intercollege sports were fast becoming big business in the United States. Under the pressures of this competition some schools had been subsidizing athletes and juggling entrance and other published academic requirements. In my first address after taking office as President I expressed my views to a group of my colleagues in other universities. Athletic games, I insisted, should be student affairs—as they had been in earlier days—and should now be given back to the students. After the meeting I remarked to a reporter that I was disappointed to have aroused no real discussion. The irreverent explanation was: "Dr. Ruthven, as far as your audience was concerned, you might as well have kicked the crucifix."

On returning to Ann Arbor after the talk I discussed the situation with the Board of Regents. I insisted that sports should not be operated as a money-making business but as recreation and physical education. Athletes should not be bought and academic standards should be upheld. The Regents did not agree that the trend toward professionalism was as serious and inevitable as it seemed to me. We agreed, however, in having confidence in the ideals and integrity of the men who were directing our programs, and I was to express to the staff the hope that unfortunate trends toward overemphasis could by precept and example be stemmed.

In almost twenty years I found little to criticize in the effectiveness and co-operation of the officials in the registrar's and in the Association offices. Academic standards were maintained, the number of contests was limited, no postseason games were played, and no charity games were allowed (even when requested by an irate governor). With full confidence in our officials I early resigned from the Board of Intercollegiate Athletics.

In the years following I continued to observe signs of creeping professionalism in the nation's schools. In spite of protestations of purity, evidence accumulated that students refused admission to Michigan were admitted to sister institutions, sometimes with substantial stipends. I even had the record of a young athlete who was admitted to a sister institution before graduating from high school. This lad played on the college teams for four years and failed each year to meet the published academic requirements.

As competition increased rivalry for promising young athletes increased. Procurement efforts were stepped up, there was more pressure for "athletic scholarships," stadia were enlarged, and commercial interests entered the "Bowl" business.

When one surveys the whole scene, the situation becomes obvious. In some schools academic requirements (as enforced although often not as published) are absurdly low for athletes. More and larger athletic scholarships are available. Bowl games, all star games, and charity games extend the football season practically through the first semester. Cases of bribery are uncovered. More and more emphasis is placed in intercollegiate sports on developing the talents of the few—the best players. In short, the schools have become to some extent inexpensive farm clubs for the professional leagues.

I am sure that most people watching a professional game in any sport must feel today—as I do—that the participants are not playing for fun or for Detroit, Chicago, or Philadelphia, but like trained seals—for fish. Are the colleges encouraging in our students the same reaction to intercollegiate athletics? I hope not, but I am not sure. I enjoy team play and appreciate its educational values. At any rate professionalism in college athletics is now coming into the open, encouraged by commercial and gambling interests. It can be scotched, not by directors and coaches, but only by the faculties.

DAILY PROBLEMS

Someone has suggested that we should live dangerously. For a state university president, as I have said, this advice is quite superfluous. He does not know any other kind of life. There are many satisfactions to be derived from the work of directing the operations of the institution, but there are always battles to be fought in which the chief executive should be in front of and not behind the lines. His must be the head which peers over the college walls, a target for all sorts of missiles not infrequently hurled by the press, alumni, parents, organizations of various kinds, football fans, members of the legislature, and others who seem to feel that it is always open season on the schools.

If a professor makes a comment or expresses a point of view which displeases someone he is interpreted as voicing a "university policy." He may be an expert in his field and his critics quite ignorant of the matter discussed, but his head should be removed, or the faculty should be purged, with the president as "lord high executioner."

Is Johnny so dumb or indolent that it is a waste of time and money to keep him in school—the university should be able to make a silk purse, even though the parents have failed miserably. The chief executive should himself accept responsibility for the success of this operation.

When Mary gets disciplined for a misdemeanor, she is often smart enough to get her story home earlier than can the university authorities. She may also be trusted to dress up her version in ways which reflect credit on herself. Hence, her prejudiced relatives seldom fail to decide that the whole institution is out of step. The university authorities should see that she is exceptional (in the right direction, of course), no matter what her record may be.

The football team will usually win or lose each contest. When it loses, there is something rotten nearer than Denmark. The entrance requirements are too high, the training is faulty, there is trouble on the team, the coach is losing his grip, and so *ad infinitum*. When the season is successful, there are murmurings about pipe courses, low standards of admission, and subsidization, or a demand for postseason games. It does not seem to occur to many fans that for most spectators athletic contests are an emotional release and nothing else, that the game is being played by boys, and that one team must win and one must lose, except in the rare case of a tie.

Then there is the student paper. If our embryo journalists write about anything but the weather, they are certain to offend someone, and their effusions will be credited to their instructors or to lack of control by "the administration." Every president and dean of students knows that the only way the faculty or the administration could even be reasonably sure that nothing silly, libelous, or in bad taste appeared in print would be to put both students and paper to bed each night at an early hour.

The president seems to be a particularly attractive target for those who "have a screw loose." These unfortunates seem to consider him either an enemy or a kindred spirit. He is often inclined to share their latter opinion, particularly at the end of a busy day. Whatever the grievance, however, there is one sure way for those who become irritated at a college to relieve their feelings. It is to write to the president, sadly, angrily, or even abusively. If courage is lacking, the letters may be left unsigned, or better yet, an impressive pseudonym may be used. There is no reason to show consideration for his feelings or to hesitate for any other reason. He cannot fight back. He is a state employee. Presumably, also, "he can take it." His is a Procrustean bed, and, since he has agreed to occupy it, he should expect to be cut off or stretched out to fit it at the pleasure of any disgruntled citizen.

The veteran executive must suspect that he does not see all the mail addressed to him. If he has, as I had, an experienced and dedicated secretary he may be quite sure that the letters on his desk are often only those judged fit for him to read. He will appreciate this effort to keep his feelings from being unnecessarily harrowed, but he should occasionally, at least, see the productions of the pens or more often the pencils of these ready letter writers.

The following letter was written apparently by a youngster with an investigative turn of mind:

"Dear Sire. I have look in your pool by the bell tour for fish many time but some was not there, then after a downporing rain last sat. I looked agin and little black fishs was swimming a s nise a you plese. DID your workkmen put in the m minnies or did they rain in there. My ma says fish and forgs rain outa t he sky sometimes but PA dont beleve a dame bit off it. YOURS TRULY   bill sutter."

"What the devil is the matter with the administration of this University, anyhow? Teaching Jap language—and Russian —when so many of the students cannot speak good English! Read the Daily, whose editors are supposedly, at least, better than average, and note the use of "who" instead of "whom," "I" instead of "me," and other inexcusable errors.

"Like the auto manufacturers, you have fought preparedness for a war everyone of anything like sound judgment knew was coming, and now see the mess we are in.

"Get hep to yourself. Veritas."

"Gentlemen: Do you have any course in your college which teaches a person how to bet intelligently on horse races? I mean by that how to bet in a way that a person wins more money than he loses. I understand there is such a system but I don't seem able to get the correct information on it. I lose a good deal more money than I win, in the long run.

"I understand you have home-study courses, and would like to know the charges for your horse-race betting course in case you have one. It would seem that you ought to as many people lose a lot of money on horse racing and it would be a public service to show them how to win money instead of losing it.   Jack Westfield."

"My dear Mr. Dean: In view of the present world impact, I can visualize the tremendous problems that will confront the medical profession. Unfortunately, I feel that thousands upon thousands of our boys will return from the jungles of the Pacific and the typhus-ridden lands of North Africa, their poor bodies racked through the ravages of malaria, typhoid, and other tropical diseases.

"I am sure that the medical colleges of today will encourage the intensive research by medical students of this subject so as to cope with the problem in question.

"I wish I were a very wealthy man in which event I would place at the disposal of the medical colleges large and substantial sums to encourage the research necessary to the adequate solution to this problem. Not being so fixed financially, however, I can but make a modest contribution in my humble way to foster increased interest in this subject.

"To this end, I want to assign $2,500.00 worth of N.Y.C. & St. L.R.R. 4½% bonds due in 1978, which form the nucleus of a fund to be known as . . . and the income of which, viz., $112.50 annually to be offered as a prize or prizes to be decided upon by you or your Board of Trustees in a manner best calculated to encourage concentrated effort on this subject by medical students.

"If this meets with your sympathetic approval, I should like to consummate this matter immediately upon acceptance by your medical school of my son, whose application for admission to your medical school is now pending. I feel quite sure that he will prove to be a credit to your institution and maintain its high ideals and traditions. While his grades during his first year of college were not as good as might be hoped for, yet I believe he will progressively improve..." (signed by the father of a boy with an impossible record).

Anonymous letters, I found, are now and then to be expected—weird, complaining, virulent, threatening, or complimentary on occasion. The experienced secretary learns to identify these epistles with astonishing accuracy, sometimes, it seems, before she opens the envelopes.

In my experience unsigned letters fall into several categories. Those produced by the definitely deranged are often curious but never repulsive or amusing to those who understand them as symptoms of disease. Others are evidently written by timid souls who fear that if their identity were known they would be accused of effrontery or might arouse the ire of the recipient. Still others seem to be sent with the thought that criticism and threats will appear to represent a wider spread of opinion if signed "a taxpayer," "a parent," or "an alumnus."

During my regime I received relatively few such communications, judging by the experiences of some of my colleagues. One which I remember in particular was a "black hand" letter stating that my son was to be kidnapped if I did not do something or other which I have forgotten. The amusing feature of this communication was that the imprint was of a woman's hand. Our son was six feet one inch tall and a rugged athletic youngster. We felt that only an Amazon could have accomplished the feat.

Like everyone else the incumbent of the presidential chair in an institution of higher learning has his embarrassing moments. Some of these which recur with surprising frequency take place in dealing with the cases of sons and daughters of good old alumni who exhibit little relationship to their parents in their college records or general behavior, or both. The course of these events is often a notice to the parents from the dean's office, a letter from the irate parents to the president, an examination of the student record by the chief executive, a letter from him to father or mother which satisfies no one, and, finally, a call at the president's office, which is consistently anything but pleasant.

The complaints are always about the same, and the discussions uniformly seriously handicapped by the inability of the president to be quite frank in his comments. "The instructors cannot be as effective as those of the good old days." "The school must be becoming so large that the student is lost in the shuffle." "Professor A. is unfair." Always in some way the instructor must be to blame. The president must be tactful, but it is difficult not to suggest sometimes that the youngster may have been spoiled in the making. Again, a father cannot safely be reminded that son or daughter may in some ways take after the mother's side of the house. It is equally hard and dangerous to call to the attention of a mother that, while she may be a Phi Beta Kappa, her other half possibly possesses something less than her brilliancy. She probably knows the score, but desires to keep it dark.

The ordeal of the interview cannot be avoided and must be borne without even the relief of a grin. At the best it is embarrassing and, if the family has been a donor or had a regent, the president's face may be really red as he listens to all of the things which a disappointed parent can say.

I found the only course to take in these delicate situations was to pour on the troubled waters whatever oil was handy, being careful that it was not ignited by any suggestion that either the parents or the instructors were to blame. If the disaster could be attributed to "the times," or earlier schooling, there was a chance that the interview could be terminated with a minimum of bitterness. This was often a forlorn hope. There would seem to be but one way to effect a general solution to this problem and to avoid embarrassment to all parties. The method is herewith proposed as a new procedure in education.

All parents should be required to take a course in genetics before sending their children to college. They should learn that their young hopefuls inherit from both sides of the house. They should learn that the chips are not off just one of the old blocks, but from a tree that may have many defective parts. Having learned the story of the genes, they could wage in the home the battle of who is to blame for the shortcomings of John or Jane rather than carry to the college campus what should be a domestic war.

I have never agreed with some college presidents that the position permits the incumbent to delegate responsibility which should be borne by the president, to give addresses for payment, or to take part in outside activities which promise to enhance his prestige but interfere with the work he is expected to do for his institution.

Possibly due in part to knowledge of my own limitations I made it a practice not to accept payment for speeches given to any organization. The few times when it would have been embarrassing not to accept offered stipends I placed the funds in a university trust fund to be used in emergencies to assist students. This fund was augmented by Christmas presents from alumni who learned of it. It was very satisfying to be able to give needy students a lift from this fund when such small gifts often made the difference between remaining in or withdrawing from the University.

For me the position of president was a full-time job of seven days a week, including many nights.

During the war a distinguished general called me one morning and asked me to come to Washington and supervise the allocation of steel to industries in this country and to our allies. I laughed, which I should not have done, and hastened to apologize. I told him the University was making a large contribution to the war effort, including the installation of several new training programs, and there were serious staff problems involving both the engaging of many additional instructors for the new programs and the replacement of men being called for duty elsewhere. He remarked impatiently that he did not think this an excuse. I could come to Washington and still run the University with my left hand. This, in turn, irritated me. I had to tell him very plainly that mine was not a part-time job and that I found it difficult to run the University well with two hands! This ended the discussion, but the general I am sure never forgave me. I could also have told him that what I did not know about the manufacture and distribution of steel would have filled a large book if not a library of respectable size.

Only those who lived through the depression of the early 1930's can realize the tensions which the members of staff sustained during that period. The closing of the banks, the wiping out of many investments and accumulated savings, and the uncertainty that salaries would be paid were disquieting situations for people on relatively small stipends. Fortunately, my relations with the Ann Arbor bankers gave me some knowledge of what was going on in the financial world and enabled me to assist in reorganizing the local banks. I informed the staff that I had sufficient confidence in the future to deposit my salary in the local institutions, and this I believe helped to forestall runs on the Ann Arbor banks.

The University was able to avoid all but one payless payday and that failure was only a brief postponement. Of course, during the bank holiday no checks could be issued by the state treasurer, but thanks to the efforts of an efficient University comptroller we succeeded in getting the monies as needed. Just before a payday he, with a member of the sheriff's office, would go to Lansing with a suitcase, make the rounds of the state offices which were receiving payments from various sources, and collect the nickels, dimes, pennies, and dollars in the tills. The cash would be brought back to Ann Arbor, where he and his assistants would spend the night sorting and counting it.

I must here pay tribute to the staff who, when salaries and wages elsewhere had to be cut, insisted that whether the money was available or not they also should have reductions in their stipends.

From my museum days I had been convinced that the educational activities of the University as a state institution should extend beyond the campus. I was confirmed in this opinion during World War II, when the British government asked me to come to England and Scotland. My mission was to give such advice and counsel as I could to the educational authorities and Parliament on future plans for education in Great Britain. My secretary insists I never read all of the letter of invitation from the British Embassy, for as soon as I noted its import I wired I was ready to go at any time.

I took off on a British plane secretly about 2:30 one morning. The old British ship rattled at every joint. I was not uneasy that it would not hold together until, off Newfoundland, the pilot and copilot both came back to visit with me. When I asked them who was up front they said no one for the moment, but not to worry because the plane flew better when nobody was fooling with it. I didn't know whether to believe them or not.

I had a delightful traveling companion on the trip, also a guest of the British government, Fred Allen, editor of *Harper's Magazine*. We landed at Southampton and proceeded to London by train arriving in the blackout—an awesome experience for the uninitiated.

The bombing was supposed to be about over, which I regretted only because, as I said before leaving, I had hoped to have the experience of going through one attack. The Germans accommodated me by bombing London every night I was there.

The first night in London I stepped through the blackout curtains in the hotel to see what was going on. When I saw the first German plane shot down flaming to earth and thought of the young fellows in the holocaust, I had a greater realization than ever before of the stupidity and uselessness of war. Why try to educate youth for a better world order if we are not to have one? Are we to believe those psychologists who insist we cannot educate the beast out of man? I once argued that the only excuse for war in human society would be cannibalism.

As I was standing on the pavement in the dark, puzzled by the tinkling noises all about me, a hand reached out from a black doorway and drew me inside. I rather irritatedly asked what it was all about. An English policemen said, "My lad, don't you realize that is shrapnel?" I was too depressed even to thank him for misjudging my age. I returned to my room and wrote a letter to my little granddaughter, the first paragraph of which read:

"Dear Sandra, This is your first letter from London and it is being written while antiaircraft guns are booming like thunder. I hope when you are grown up this terrible foolishness is looked upon for what it is—just plain barbarism. I do not want you to have to listen to the scream of a bomb . . . Buzz."

I soon became familiar with the austere conditions under which my British friends were living, and the calm, deliberate way in which they were "carrying on." The scanty food supplies, the cold houses, the great gaps where large buildings once stood, beautiful churches with only a wall remaining, the mountains of rubble in the parks, the hordes of children herded in community kitchens for their one nourishing meal for the day, the sound of exploding bombs, antiaircraft guns, and sirens at night, and the depressing blackouts were all accepted as a part of the business of "getting on with the job." To the visiting scientist-teacher the waste, the destruction of young lives, and the sacrifices represented a reversion to a stage of society which "civilized" peoples should have left far behind.

I was most interested in the efforts the English were making to continue adult education even under the distressing conditions. Night after night I was taken into basements, often in partly bombed buildings, to listen to instruction on all sorts of subjects. The classes were for the most part conducted by university tutors.

My father and his family had come from Scotland, and I wanted to see their old home as well as to continue gathering information on adult teaching in Edinburgh and Glasgow. Just before going to those cities, however, I spent a few days with instructors in adult courses in Lincoln, where most of the students were workers in munition plants.

In Lincoln I became acquainted with the dean of the famous cathedral and, having become indebted to him, yielded to his invitation to address his congregation at a Sunday morning service. I returned to London to find that the minister of Information was trying to reach me. When I called on him, he said, "Well, we had lost track of you until we noted that you had preached in the cathedral in Lincoln. This is the first time to my knowledge that a biologist has ever occupied the pulpit in an English cathedral." I assured him that it was the first and last time for me. I was scared then and remained scared.

His reason for calling was a message from Scotland. Authorities there had heard that a Ruthven was in England on an educational mission. They would like to know if my name was really Ruthven. If so they urged very strongly that I come to

Scotland. It was apparent that with their usual clannishness the Scots were not interested in me unless I was one of them. As I had had this experience before when attending scientific meetings in Scotland, I was not surprised. Neither, of course, were my English friends.

Both in Scotland and England I was greatly aided in my work by two old friends. The president of the University of Glasgow, Sir Hector Hetherington, and his staff gave me every possible assistance, as did the vice-chancellor of Oxford University, Alexander Lindsay, later Lord Lindsay, who was a leader in adult education in Great Britain.

I returned to the United States an enthusiastic advocate of "continuing education" and a promoter of our Extension Service and other state efforts to meet the educational needs of the older generations. With a special appropriation from the legislature the University initiated a pilot program in worker education, only to have it sabotaged in a short time, as related, by an "economic royalist."

I have never ceased to be grateful for the opportunity to observe the British program of worker education. It was my privilege to visit classes in munition plants, hospitals, military centers, and small and large towns. I could have gone to few of these meetings in the blackout without the guides provided by the Ministry of Education and the universities.

The students represented a wide variety of occupations. I met dock workers, crane operators, housewives, hospital maids, potterymakers, and others, including some professional men and women. The classes selected the subjects to be considered. The teachers were supplied by the universities, and the teaching was by the discussion method. I was privileged to take part in the programs, much more, I am sure, to my edification than to the benefit of the students.

At or even before the end of each course the members voted on retaining the instructor or requesting a new one. On one occasion I attended the final meeting of a course. After the class was dismissed the students and the instructor retired to a nearby "pub." Here over a tankard of ale they discussed seriously and frankly their evaluations of the course, the next subject to be studied, and the qualifications of their instructor. The wartime ale wasn't very good. The discussion was most interesting, pleasant, and instructive. At one point I listened with great interest to an intelligent discussion of the scientific method of evaluating data by crane operators, housewives, and others engaged in common labor.

It still seems strange to me that in our boasted system of public education in the United States an important group of citizens is denied the advantages of "continuing education." The bugaboo of possible "indoctrination" still plagues both labor and management.

As a state university president I soon discovered that I was supposed to have a talk prepared for every occasion. I had, however, no desire to be known as a speechmaker. Unlike President Burton, who often said that if there were speeches to be made he preferred to make them, I never enjoy preparing or giving talks and only occasionally do I enjoy listening to them.

On occasion I found that I was expected to be available as a pinch hitter when programs went awry. Once I had direct evidence of this.

The telephone invitation was most flattering. The people of the state were pleased with my administration. The invitation was being given on behalf of a community very anxious to meet me and by an organization the members of which had been impressed with my pronouncements on social problems. The invitation was too flattering. I could not remember when I had made any earth-shaking pronouncements on social problems. When I learned that I was wanted the next day, I was sure other considerations had probably prompted the invitation. I asked quickly why the haste and, without thinking, my caller blurted out, "Miss Addams was to be here but has broken a leg."

I always felt obligated to attend—when I could—meetings of our alumni clubs. These were usually at a dinner and entailed an after-dinner talk. My first experiences were with the New York City club, and they were rather disturbing. The custom had been for a number of years to have the President's talk carefully timed to finish just as the Broadway theaters were closing. At the conclusion of the talk the doors would be flung open and the chorus from some musical show would take over. The competition was too great. I never could be sure whether the alumni were listening to me or just waiting for the curtain to go up on the main show. After a harrowing experience, I asked that this type of program be discontinued.

My talk concluded, I had to dash for a train. The toast-master showed me a side door through which I could make an inconspicuous exit. I slipped through the door only to find my-self in the midst of a bevy of scantily clad beauties preparing to enter the banquet hall. The girls didn't seem to mind the in-trusion, but I was certain it was no place for a college president or Mrs. Ruthven's husband. I fled through the kitchen.

One of our alumni dinners had a tragic aftermath. The president of the local club, a successful and likeable man but very modest, had a real dread of being in the public eye. It took much persuasion by the alumni to get him to preside on this occasion. I tried to encourage him throughout the dinner, which was for him an ordeal. At the end of the program as we were leaving the room, I said, "Now that wasn't too hard was it?" He fell dead at my feet. No one ever remembered my message at this meeting.

To my surprise I soon became disillusioned with com-mencement addresses by invited speakers. I discovered that not a few of them—even those of our most distinguished guests—

were apparently written on the train on the way to Ann Arbor, occasionally even after the speaker had arrived. My secretary remarked more than once when she received the manuscripts in advance for transmittal to the newsmen, "Here is another talk not worth what we paid for it."

I spent much time preparing my talks, rewriting the manuscripts over and over again, as I would a scientific paper. From time to time friends, recognizing the amount of work this entailed, suggested that I let them at least rough out ideas I might want to express. I experimented with a ghostwriter just once and became convinced that thereafter I would have to do my own chores in this field.

As a college president known to be interested in religious education I occasionally could not refuse requests to occupy a pulpit. This was an especially trying experience. Trained as a scientist to be as brief as possible, I was always sure my messages sounded more like technical papers than sermons. They probably did. Be this as it may, I never overcame a feeling of inadequacy when I faced a church audience whether in a small country church or in a large cathedral.

The first time I tried to perform as a "minister of the gospel" was in a large old church in Detroit. The audience was distinguished and very polite, but I felt from the beginning that I was not getting close to my listeners. I became more disturbed when I saw women ducking their heads and heard murmurs of apprehension. The cause of the uneasiness soon became apparent. It was not my performance. A bat seemingly felt more at home in the church than I did. This emergency was in my field. Interrupting my discourse, I gave a two-minute talk on bats, assuring the ladies that while they might have "rats" they would never find bats in their hair. It wasn't much of a joke, but in the laughter that followed the ice was broken, and we got along better.

The colored minister was an agreeable fellow and a friend of mine. He was so pleasant in fact that one usually purchased tickets for his church functions with a minimum of pain, often even without realizing what was happening. When he asked me to officiate at a service, the invitation was so sugar-coated that acceptance followed as a matter of course.

On the appointed Sunday morning I found myself in the pulpit facing a larger congregation than I had expected. The preliminaries proceeded in the usual sequence until the collection was called for, marred only by the circumstance that I had not been told I was to read the Scripture lesson. Fortunately, the Bible was open on the lectern at the thirteenth chapter of Jeremiah, which as I remembered began appropriately enough for a lesson. All unwittingly I began the reading at the fifteenth verse only to wobble painfully and finally stall before I reached the twenty-third verse. Needless to say, it was an embarrassing situation.

When the minister called for the morning offering the ushers gathered the plates and proceeded to pass them in the orthodox fashion, except that at the head of each aisle under the eagle eye of the minister stood a sister with a large handbag. At intervals an usher would hold a bill high in the air and then hurry to the altar to have it changed by one of the holders of a handbag. Noticing my curiosity, the minister explained in a whisper: "Our people like to impress their neighbors. If they have a bill they will pretend that this is the smallest they have. In an earlier day they got away with it, for the ushers could rarely make change. I put an end to this. We now have the change for any bill likely to be offered, but we never have any coins for change smaller than a quarter. The brothers may display their wealth if they care to do so, but if they yield to temptation, as they will, they must pay the church for the privilege."

I felt less miscast than usual in the role of a preacher. It was a village church and in the congregation were a number of my neighbors. I had a theme which I thought was suitable for the occasion and would be of interest to my listeners. In short, I felt reasonably at ease. When I rose to speak, however, I was startled to see sitting solemnly in a row in the middle of the church my son, whom I knew was critical of some of my ideas, and the three friends whom I probably least expected to see in all the world—a prominent industrialist, the director of our Museum of Classical Archeology, and a distinguished Oxford don. It was too late to change even the text of my so-called sermon, which in their presence seemed inappropriate.

One discourse given in a church apparently had a curious result. A mousy little girl, quiet and serious, announced that the reason for her visit to my office was important to her. She had heard my talk and had been inspired to bring me a message. Even a hardened president may be flattered to hear that a student seeks an interview to commend an address he has given. Evidently, some of the seed painstakingly sown had fallen on fertile ground. Now for the harvest. I was not kept in suspense. Evidently, I had not recognized the lady, which was not surprising since she was fully clothed even if possibly not in her right mind. She was by her own admission none other than the reincarnation of our apple-loving grandmother Eve. There was a tense moment, but it passed in safety. Her business was not to bring forbidden fruit or to introduce a serpent to a herpetologist. It was to offer safety from the wrath to come by one who saw the world today as a vast Sodom and Gomorrah. Not only was I chosen to be saved, but I was to have a front seat at the forthcoming holocaust. The Creator had given up. His creatures had failed to justify their existence. It was time for a really "new deal."

This news was not as disturbing as it might have been,

since I was to be saved, but the details were confusing. Eve was not alone to have the responsibility for the very few brands to be plucked from the burning. Adam was to share her burden. He had been detained on Mars until February 15. The reason for his detention on that planet was not clear, but in general it appeared that the Martians had been behaving about as badly as the earth people and were in the process of being liquidated. (Our space travelers might investigate this.)

Here was food for thought. Would life on a globe depopulated except for Adam, his consort, and me be attractive enough to be worthwhile? However, was it wise to refuse salvation on any terms? Could one discover any significance for education in the fact that the lady had an excellent scholastic record? Had the President's speech which prompted the interview really placed him in the way of being saved, or had it contributed to the breakdown of a student? Alas, these questions were to remain unanswered.

On the pretext of wanting all the information I would need in order to be prepared for the millennium I invited "Eve" to continue her visits to the office. In the meantime I asked the dean of women to cultivate the girl's friendship and see if she could gain her confidence. For weeks after the first visit the dean assured me from time to time that the girl was seemingly perfectly normal, had no interest in Eve or in Adam, and continued to maintain excellent standings in her courses. At long last however the dean did gain her confidence to the extent that she also was offered a chance to be saved. We were then able to get the student into a hospital. It has always been a matter of pleasure to me that she ultimately made a complete recovery, attained an important position, and finally had no recollection of her temporary delusions—or were they delusions?

I was never under any illusions as to my abilities as a speechwriter or speechmaker. Before coming to the presidency I had

had years of training by teachers and editors of scientific publications in saying what I had to say in the fewest words possible. My talks thus had at least one virtue, an attribute appreciated by most audiences—they made up in brevity what they may have lacked in wit.

Long introductions distress me. I always tried to forestall them—sometimes without success. They not only embarrassed me, but occasionally made me suspicious that the introducer was seizing the opportunity to express his own opinions on what I might, or should, talk about. On one occasion nature intervened to interrupt what promised to be a lengthy presentation.

The toastmaster was a distinguished citizen in his community. He loved the sound of his own voice. He had strong opinions on almost everything, including education. Out of respect for his position people were accustomed to listening to him and overlooking his dogmatism. I noted when he started to introduce me that he was all wound up and on his way to making a longer speech than I intended to make. He was in full cry when a minor earth tremor jarred the building. Everyone was startled, including the speaker, who stopped in the middle of a sentence and sat down. I only needed to thank him for an earth-shaking introduction.

During my first ten years in office, I found that state schools in Michigan in defending their requests before the legislative committees were making the task unnecessarily difficult and confusing. Often their independent and even secret presentations gave the impression that they were in conflict. Now and then, undoubtedly, they were. Also, at times, members of the legislature were not averse to playing one school against another.

After studying the matter, I proposed to the presidents of the several state colleges that we form a council which would meet each year to discuss our needs frankly before presenting budget requests to the lawmakers. In time this council developed a splendid spirit of co-operation. At first, I'm quite sure, we "played our cards close to our vests," but we soon learned that we could arrive at common understandings and mutual appreciation of the needs of the different institutions and work together.

It always seemed to me that voluntary co-operation between the schools is a better method of co-ordinating their activities than regimentation under a single board. Failure of presidents to work together presents a problem for the trustees. It is the business of governing boards to get executives who aspire to be educators as well as administrators.

The plan of a single state board looks well on an organization chart. It does not follow from this, however, that it is the best method of encouraging the schools to experiment with— and to develop as they should—new and improved programs. If the experience of the schools with federally supported programs in education is a criterion, it would appear to be inevitable that under a single state board the institutions will find themselves sooner or later operating under a dictator, or even worse, under clerks whose chief interest would usually be in multiplying rules and regulations to make their jobs appear important.

To perform and function properly the institutions must, of course, be well organized, with teaching and research the business of the faculty, administration the business of the president and the staff, and corporate responsibilities the business of the trustees. In these days of large and growing schools with millions in endowments, extensive physical plants, and numerous training programs, there are corporate responsibilities that require the services of a board of trustees for each of the larger institutions. Anyone familiar with the operation of our modern universities will recognize that the responsibilities of trustees are numerous and exacting. In these changing institutions new problems in securing funds for additional personnel, operating expenses, and educational programs should be solved with a minimum of delay. Without becoming involved in the details of administration trustees should be in such close touch with their schools that they can at all times be satisfied that the administrative staff is efficient and that the educational needs as presented by the staff are met. These responsibilities are time-consuming and require careful study.

The complaint often heard of duplication of effort in the present system of higher education in Michigan is largely witless and pointless. One might as logically object to duplication in the automobile industry because the companies all produce cars and have assembly lines.

In short, absentee management under the plan of an overall board in control cannot give the freedom to our institutions that they need and have so long enjoyed under the plan of separate boards. A single board, in my thinking, means ultimately not only government by clerks, but also discouragement of teachers and mediocrity in instruction. The plan is no better than, and possibly a step toward, federal control. I have even heard the thought expressed a few times that perhaps the difficulty in securing adequate funds for higher education indicates that state-supported schools should be nationalized and operated by one bureau. What a depressing suggestion!

It may be that the appointment of a co-ordinator serving a council of presidents could be of some advantage in organizing budget requests to the legislature. I have considerable doubt, however, that it would be altogether a wise procedure. If it were left to the co-ordinator to present the budgets, the legislative committees would be inclined to consider him a professional lobbyist. If his task were merely to show the schools how to eliminate unnecessary duplication, it may properly be asked who can do this better than the officers of the several institutions working together to promote the cause of higher education in the state?

As a museum curator I had acquired a respect for the so-called "nonacademic" employees—an appreciation that continued and increased throughout the years. These men and women operate the physical plant and the business offices, keep the records, register the students, and perform the many other services essential to the successful operation of the University. I found these staff members with very few exceptions efficient, co-operative, and interested in the University. This is, of course, to be expected of trained employees, but it seemed to me the services they performed were not always fully appreciated on the campus.

I was frequently distressed by the unjust and often absurd criticisms of the nonacademic staff by faculty members. "The grass is mowed too often." "Materials can be purchased more cheaply elsewhere than they can be supplied by the Buildings and Grounds Department." "The officials are hiring too much help." "The Business Office is running the University by controlling the funds." I have even heard a secretary accused of inefficiency when she could not find a document that never existed. To mention these criticisms is to reveal how absurd they are. One suspects that they are usually simply the product of rumor and gossip and should not be taken seriously.

Every executive soon learns to appreciate a good secretary. Her praises have been sung many times. One of my early experiences of her value occurred when I was a department chairman.

As a department head I had become irritated with a dean because he couldn't see something my way and had written him a harsh letter. A few months later he died and in talking to his secretary I expressed my sincere regret that I had written as I had.

"Never mind, Dr. Ruthven," she said. "He never saw the letter. I knew it would hurt him, and you would sometime regret sending it."

When I took over the curatorship of the Museum there were very few telephones on the campus and none in my office. They were hard to come by and much desired. After I secured one a covetous department head persuaded the Business Office that he needed the facility more than did the Museum. The first I knew of the matter was when I returned from lunch one day and found my secretary, who probably weighed all of eighty-five pounds, sitting on the telephone facing two burly mechanics, defying them to attempt to move her. The instrument remained.

I shall not attempt to express my indebtedness to the secretary who served with me throughout my term as President. She was courteous to visitors of all kinds, firm but respectful to the faculty, and kind and sympathetic to the students. She once told me that she had one rule in regard to my office appointments. "Students get in first, faculty members second, and deans when they can."

This was a "rule" made to be broken in emergencies, but the expression was an indication of her belief, as it was mine, that the University should be a human institution and not an assembly line. With it all, she had an amazing knowledge of the operations of the University and of campus personalities. Almost daily she facilitated my work and not infrequently kept me out of trouble.

I have had the thought now and then that it would be an interesting experiment, if it were not too expensive, to let the faculty try operating the plant for a time. As for me, I am glad to acknowledge the great debt of gratitude I owe to the members of the nonacademic staff for the assistance I received from them throughout my career as an administrator.

THE LEGISLATURE

For ten years as President I was satisfied that the Michigan method of electing regents was a good one. Those familiar with the history of state politics in the next decade will understand why I changed my mind. Sufficient to say, the position of regent became of political importance. Some men became candidates for nomination who had little interest in higher education, but were assets to their party. Persons who would have made good regents were often not nominated because they were not active party workers. As a consequence, the field of qualified candidates was narrowed.

To me the most promising alternative to the popular election of trustees for the state universities, if the positions are to be kept out of the political arena, is appointment by the governor with confirmation by the Senate. This method was unanimously recommended by the committee on Ferris Institute and the Wayne University commission. It was adopted by the legislature for Ferris but was rejected for Wayne, principally, as I was privately informed by a prominent senator, "to embarrass the governor." How silly can one get in politics?

One chore the president of a state school can never neglect is the task of convincing the legislature each year that he knows what is best for his school. The task is usually difficult, often frustrating, not seldom irritating, and over a period of years discouraging. Various factors account for these difficulties. Budget requests invariably far exceed the funds *considered* available. Legislators more often than not come to the sessions uninformed of the nature of the schools they are supposed to support, and they often do not remain long enough in office to learn what they need to know to arrive at competent judgments. The lawmakers are also bedeviled constantly by clever and "well-heeled" lobbyists of powerful interests and by demands of their constituents. Finally, they soon find if they have political aspirations they must be contented to become serfs to the party whips.

A president once in a moment of discouragement called the members of the legislative bodies in his state "stupid." This is an unjustified generalization. Legislators are individuals. They may be uninformed, narrow-minded, or subservient to particular interests, but they are seldom stupid. When I have watched them in action I have often recalled the observation of the Spanish philosopher, freely translated: We are all as God made us and some of us even worse.

I would be less than frank if I gave the impression that all was sweetness and light in my work with the legislature. At times my patience was sorely tried. It was particularly frustrating that some matters were perennial subjects of controversy which had bedeviled my predecessors and bade fair to trouble my successors.

Year after year I had to try to explain to some of our legislators the advantages to Michigan students and to the state of Michigan of admitting out-of-state, including foreign, students. The Michigan idea has, as I have interpreted it, always been that it is educationally sound to admit out-of-state students, that the number of these students should be under control, and this control should be exercised by the University. If this policy is ever changed Michigan will not be the University that it has been up to this time. Regardless of the number of students it will become a provincial school.

Through the years the University of Michigan has fared fairly well in its support from the state. This has been due in part to the efforts of its officials in presenting its objectives and needs. Its steady progress has, however, been mostly made possible by the form of organization set up by its founders. Its strength over a considerable period of time has been its constitutional status. To this date it has been a fourth arm of state government. This position has given the Board of Regents sole responsibility for its activities and full custodianship of its funds. It has been a bulwark against all attempts of politicians or others to dictate policies and programs. I learned this early as President.

One of the governors of the state had launched a vicious attack on the institution. With some concern I started to discuss the matter at a Board meeting. There was no evidence of concern. This troubled me for a few minutes. Then one of the Regents, a Catholic, remarked dryly, "Mr. President, never forget, in Michigan the Board of Regents is higher than the Pope."

An advantage which the University enjoyed for many years was the mill-tax method of support adopted by the legislature. This gave a continuing base for the appropriations, although it did not entirely relieve the University officials of the task of requesting aid from Lansing. With the growing population of the state, the increasing enrollments, and the rising costs of education the percentage of the mill-tax from time to time had to be "increased." It had also been the custom to use mill-tax funds for operations and to ask for separate appropriations for capital expenditures. Unfortunately, in the course of time the state property tax was abandoned, and the University was compelled to receive its funds by direct appropriation.

Another handicap in working with legislatures arose when the sessions were changed from biennial to annual. On the biennial plan it had been possible and certainly profitable for the University to plan ahead. The officials had a year between sessions when they did not have to spend an inordinate amount of time educating the senators and representatives. The task now is a continuing and harrowing one.

I early adopted several methods of dealing with Lansing. I insisted that the Ways and Means Committee of the House and the Finance Committee of the Senate visit the University during the sessions as many times as I could get them. Also once a session, following the custom of my predecessors, I had the entire legislature at the University for a day. The Ann Arbor visits became more difficult to arrange after the legislature began to meet annually.

At the meetings it was possible to demonstrate the University's activities and needs and to draw out questions the legislators had which might not otherwise have come to our attention. One experience I record because it illustrates the importance of learning and quietly counteracting unfounded rumors and impressions.

At a meeting of the legislature in Ann Arbor a new representative from northern Michigan was present, who had been very vocal in criticism of the University. Early in the session he had read an item in a Detroit newspaper facetiously commenting on a study being made by one of the professors on "waltzing mice." He was so excited about this item that he had secured copies of the paper and given them to each of his colleagues. I ignored his attacks.

When the group was assembled at Ann Arbor I introduced my talk by pointing out that the University was a very complex institution. I hoped the members would clear with us whenever they had any doubts as to work that was being done on the campus. I pointed out as an example of something that might have puzzled them the report on the professor and his dancing mice. I then asked them abruptly if they had ever seen a child with epilepsy and briefly described some of the symptoms. The smiles about the room when I first mentioned the matter quickly disappeared. I told them that perhaps they had visualized a bespectacled old gentleman sitting in front of a cage of dancing mice accompanying the gyrations of his pets with a mouth organ. Actually, I explained, he thought that the peculiar trait of these animals was related to epilepsy and that if this could be established they might be good experimental material for studies leading to the treatment of the malady. I then went on to discuss the aims and objectives of the University.

At the end of a rather long session, as we were about to disband, the critical representative rose to his feet and said, "Gentlemen, I have been a fool. From now on anything the University asks I am going to vote for." I did not find out until a year or two later that his little granddaughter had the disease. I wrote him a letter of apology to which he replied that no apology was necessary, for he had needed just that lesson.

The meetings in Ann Arbor away from the turmoil of Lansing gave me and my associates a chance to answer many questions in the minds of the lawmakers and to forestall unfounded criticisms. I was often a disappointment to newsmen because I refused to answer publicly attacks made on the University by members of the legislature. I soon learned that remarks critical of the institution were often for constituents or were merely rumors and gossip. These could be answered by telephone or a personal visit—or even by a letter—without embarrassing the critic.

One method of securing appropriations often used, and certainly a tempting one, is to exaggerate needs so that if cuts are made the appropriations will still be as much as expected. I never thought this was good policy. For many years after taking office I tried to see to it—and to convince the legislature —that our requests represented actual needs. In the course of time the University gained the reputation of not inflating its budget requests.

I also held fast to a practice initiated by my predecessors

of using the appropriations for operating expenses and capital costs for the purposes for which they were made. In other words, although we could legally have done so, after getting the appropriations we did not use grants of operating funds for capital expenditures or the reverse.

Toward the close of my tenure of office I had on some occasions the pleasure of being called to Lansing ostensibly to defend our requests before the committees on finance only to be told they would be granted but the committees would like to have a visit with the President before the legislature adjourned.

But it was not always thus. I still insist that while honesty may be the best policy in dealing with the legislature, it is a ridiculous system which requires a state university president, honest or otherwise, to battle every year with smooth and well-equipped lobbyists of powerful interests for funds to support one of our most important social responsibilities. I have suggested that a better procedure would be for the legislature to appropriate a lump sum for the universities, the money to be apportioned to the several institutions by a grants committee composed of representatives of the governing boards. So far the proposal has fallen on deaf ears.

Since retirement I have often tried to evaluate my experiences in dealing with the legislature. The attempts of individual members of the House and Senate and the appropriating committees to reduce the requests of the University were mostly due to ignorance of the needs of the institution, to political considerations, or to an honest determination to "balance the state budget" (whatever that means). I cannot recall any personal attacks, even in critical periods when feelings ran high. In fact, I made many good friends in the legislature, mostly among those without absorbing political ambitions, for administrators of state schools soon discover political aspirations make feeble reeds of legislators.

When this small-time farmer, who stammered badly, came to the legislature his associates did not take him seriously. It soon became evident, however, that he was determined to learn and to meet his responsibilities. He was at first startled at the size of the requests of the state agencies. After a trying session of the Ways and Means Committee, during which he detected that I had become irritated at some of his questions, he asked me to visit him in his room in a boardinghouse. We talked briefly about the University and he then said: "Mr. President, you must be patient with me. I did not have much schooling. In my best years I never saw more than $1,500. I intend to learn." He learned. In a few years he had familiarized himself with the needs of the state departments and had become an authority on state government. He was much in demand as a speaker to school classes in spite of his speech defect and was awarded an honorary degree by the Board of Regents on the unanimous recommendation of the faculty committee on these degrees. He was a statesman.

President Angell is reported to have told the legislature after a session in which the University did not fare too well that the situation would be different in the future. Sometime more University of Michigan graduates would be elected as senators and representatives and would see to it that the needs of higher education received proper consideration. His prediction was only half right. It is true that through the years more graduates of Michigan and other universities came to the legislature, but University officials to this day encounter difficulties in getting their budget requests properly considered.

An experience with the legislature repeated all too often never failed to irritate me. In session after session some member would call for an estimate of the cost per student and would question the practice of admitting out-of-state, particularly foreign, students.

Year after year I pointed out that any general estimate of the cost per student was bound to be meaningless, and it would certainly not be to their benefit to segregate Michigan students from the rest of the world during their college years.

It was usually the claim of the critics that their concern was for the increasing costs of higher education. In time I learned that this was not always true. Often their real objectives were either to obtain a larger share of state funds for their own interests or to force the lowering of entrance requirements. These discoveries did little to keep my blood pressure at a safe level.

In a few years of experience as President I learned more about politics than I had ever absorbed in classes in political science. Among other things I discovered that it was easier to arouse active interest in higher education among the rural and labor representatives at Lansing than in the college group. The reason also became apparent. While the rural and labor representatives with some exceptions seldom had serious political ambitions, the college group was usually made up in large proportion of men with strong political aspirations. Ambitious members of the legislature learn very quickly how to become "slick" politicians, willing subjects of party discipline, and silent or vocal advocates of special interests.

It is a strong statement but I make it deliberately: Very seldom in twenty-three years could I find an alumnus in the legislature who was willing vigorously and publicly to sponsor the budget requests of the University. Our former students, while proclaiming their "loyalty" on other occasions, were usually disinclined to stand up and be counted when the going became rough.

In working with the legislature, I also soon acquired respect for the secretaries of the committees on finance. I found them to be intelligent women, loyal to their committees, but ever willing to be helpful to those to be interviewed. Not seldom, it seemed to me, they knew more about the work of the committees than did the individual members.

I was making my final appearance before one of the committees on appropriations. The discussion was on two compromise figures. Mine was, of course, the higher. My arguments finally prevailed, and the chairman sent a memorandum to his secretary. As I stopped at her desk, she showed me the note and asked if I was satisfied. I was not. The amount given was the one the committee had first proposed. I told her of the mistake and asked for another conference, whereupon she promptly settled the matter: "Never mind, Dr. Ruthven, I will change the figure. I know what the chairman feels the University should have. The rest of the committee members have by now forgotten what they voted. Let's help get this session of the legislature on the road."

EXPANSION AND BRANCHES

Through the years I heard much discussion in the faculty and elsewhere on the optimum size of the University. Obviously, large institutions offer advantages to the student that smaller schools cannot provide. The important question is at what point does growth run afoul of the law of diminishing returns. The total enrollment at the University of Michigan or at any other school is not a significant figure as far as instruction is concerned. The critical statistics, as every instructor knows, are the student-teacher ratios. These may vary widely from department to department. To be considered also are the burden on administration and the economic impact on the community of expansion of the physical plant of a growing tax-free institution. One suspects that these growth factors are sometimes ignored by administrators of state schools. The practice often seems to be to take more students as an argument for larger appropriations to permit the admission of more students, and so on indefinitely to the glory of the institution.

As early as 1906 and undoubtedly earlier, President Angell called the attention of the Regents to the need for acquiring land in excess of the forty acres comprising the original campus. He pointed out that it was unfortunate that more property wasn't available without the acquisition of private residences. He was able to expand the campus in the immediate environs and in the hospital area, and in later years the Regents continued to enlarge the University holdings.

I had not been long in office before I realized that the University should not continue to acquire residential properties within the city because of increasing costs and the effect on the town of removing property from the tax rolls. Finally, in a talk to the alumni, meant also for public notice, I expressed the opinion that provision should be made for an expansion of the University beyond the city limits of Ann Arbor. The Regents agreed and a plot was purchased to the south of Stadium Boulevard. There were, it was recognized, disadvantages in this location but it seemed the best available at the time. Fortunately, a few years later it became possible to buy properties north of Ann Arbor, a much more satisfactory site, and it was decided to extend the campus in that direction.

After my original talk several people seized on the idea that the University could expand its facilities by starting a branch in Flint. This was far from what I had suggested. As a matter of fact, I had previously resisted pressures to establish two branches in the Upper Peninsula, a branch in Grand Rapids, and to approve requests that the University take over Ferris Institute at Big Rapids. I could not bring myself to recommend to the Regents the establishment of a branch in Flint and was successful in opposing this branch for eight years.

Ironically, after the Regents established the college at Flint, shortly after my retirement, I continued to receive for several years commendation from the sponsors of the branch for initiating the idea. My opposition to the formation of branches of the institution may have been the result of a provincial attitude of mind, but it seemed to me then, as it does now, that it would be much better to organize independent colleges in desirable locations than to multiply the problems of the administrators in Ann Arbor.

At no time was I opposed to the establishment of a college in Flint. In fact, I had long been a strong proponent of community colleges with or without state support. It has been a disappointment to me that more of these schools were not organized in my time.

A part of my opposition to branches was and is that this method of meeting educational needs inevitably places increased burdens on administrative officers of the parent institution to the disadvantage of both units. Early in my time as President, I insisted that our executives should not be mere superclerks buried in routine, bosses, or gladhanders. They should maintain an active interest in the programs of the departments and in the welfare of the students and staff. As administrative responsibilities increase the institution becomes less and less a community of scholars and more and more an education factory.

It was, and is, my belief that any branch would certainly be presented with special problems which it would be able to handle best without interference. As schools are organized, they should be independent—not stepchildren of the University. That my conclusions in this area were shared by others was made clear to me in the joint legislative committee to consider the future of Ferris Institute and the large commission created to study the problems of Wayne University. As chairman of these two groups, I spent some time gathering materials that I thought the committees would need (including a large amount of correspondence paper I did not need). To my surprise both committees in our first meetings expressed themselves as being in unanimous accord that the University had fields of teaching and research which would require all of its facilities to cultivate properly, that both Ferris and Wayne had peculiar problems which could best be solved if they were independent, and that there was nothing to be gained by making these two institutions poor relatives of the University. These conclusions were reached with much less discussion than I have heard in a faculty meeting on changes in the calendar. In my judgment, which I admit has at times been faulty, the Flint branch will not reach its full potentialities as an institution of higher education serving its area and the state until someone ties off its umbilical cord.

In a large and growing institution it is difficult to maintain proper student-teacher ratios. But there are other educational disadvantages. In the same course the students may have different lecturers, different laboratory instructors and assistants, different quiz masters, and different readers of examination papers. Not a few senior undergraduates, in the periods of rapid growth at Michigan, have told me that they had spent four years in college without seeing the heads of the departments in which they had elected courses.

Without any disparagement of the scholarship or teaching ability of young instructors and teaching fellows the fragmentation of instruction does not give the student the feeling that he is a member of an integrated institution designed to assist him to become a well-rounded individual. Unless this concept is created in the first four years of college life there is little hope of building and maintaining a strong body of alumni. Generally speaking, interested alumni are made not at the graduate level but in the undergraduate years. A few years before my retirement, in my attempts to present an image of the University to former students, I noted that younger alumni of Michigan and other universities did not think of their school as their alma mater but rather as a crowded smorgasbord at which, under certain restrictions, sometimes resented, they were expected to grab what intellectual provender they could reach.

The Experimental
Process

That man may safely venture on his way,
who is so guided that he cannot stray.

THE STUDENTS

DURING THE WAR PERIOD there were naturally new and difficult student problems to be met. Those from foreign lands were
often unable to get funds from home, and arrangements had to
be made for a time to supply them with food. On occasion I
even had to assume the position of a proud father and give the
foreign student brides away at marriage ceremonies. We naturally expected that tensions would develop among our foreign
students of different races and nationalities. In World War I
there were distressing incidents of conflict between Americans
and Germans on the campus, even involving the professors. The
tensions in World War II did not become serious.

Looking out of the window during a student tea we observed two groups of Chinese and Japanese women about to
meet in front of the house. It was at the beginning of the Sino-
Japanese conflict. Mrs. Ruthven remarked that apparently the
war was about to be extended to the campus. The groups met
and engaged in vigorous discussion. Finally, they came into
the house arm in arm, each Chinese girl with a Japanese girl.
Meeting them in the hall Mrs. Ruthven asked them when the
shooting was going to start, attempting by a light remark to
soften any antagonisms. Very seriously they bowed and deliv-

ered a little speech the purport of which was that even a war should not destroy the fellowship of students engaged in securing an education.

After we entered the war the University engaged scores of Japanese instructors for the Japanese language school which the army asked us to conduct for men enlisted in various services which would require a knowledge of the language. This was the time, it will be remembered, when in other parts of the country, particularly in the Far West, the Japanese, even as United States citizens, were being herded into camps and otherwise persecuted. Any apprehension we had at the presence on the campus of many Japanese men and women instructors was soon relieved. Mrs. Ruthven and I were often amused to see groups of army personnel walking down the street chatting vigorously with Japanese instructors, men and women. On one occasion we observed two husky young soldiers seize the arms of a little Japanese woman teacher and swing her over a mud puddle much to everyone's amusement. We may be excused for believing that our student teas with the international good will they engendered had something to do with the general feeling of friendship in the student body in those trying times.

We had, as was to be expected, of course, some sad as well as pleasant experiences with the students.

A foreign student appeared at the house one afternoon terribly disturbed. The students in his dormitory, he was sure, were trying to poison him. He apparently had not eaten for some time because of this fear. We talked to him at some length and to reassure him I walked part of the way back to the dormitory with him.

I was about to take the train for a meeting in New York, but we thought we had the boy in a mental condition that his dormitory adviser could handle. That night, however, he appeared at the house again in a greatly agitated state of mind. It was up to Mrs. Ruthven to take care of him until she could get him into a hospital. This took some time because he insisted on hiding under the piano and refused to allow her to call anyone. Finally, she hit upon an individual in whom he seemed to place some trust. Fortunately, he was available, and in the late hours of the night this friend and Mrs. Ruthven were able to get the boy into the proper hands.

I was very fortunate during all of my regime to have men and women in charge of student affairs who were proficient in dealing with problems requiring student discipline. As I recall on no more than two occasions did I have to assume full responsibility.

After the war when the communist agitation was stirring the whole country, the University naturally acquired some students who claimed to be communists. Some of these young people were paid agitators, others were crackpots or fellow travelers. These students were naturally very noisy and were also prolific writers. We had little concern until a group of five or six men who were disappointed when their loud talk did not get them sufficient attention began breaking such University rules as taking liquor into the dormitories and breaking into rooms in University buildings not open to them for meetings.

I finally called this group to the office and explained to them that we had no interest in their political beliefs but that they could not violate University regulations applying to all students. When I dismissed them they went out in the hall where they had gathered some reporters and informed them that I was going to expel them from the University because they were communists. Fortunately, I heard their explanations and immediately recalled them. When I asked them why they had given out such a report and if they had not understood me they said, "Yes" they had heard me, but I had addressed them as "gentlemen" which they resented, and they lied "because this is the way we gain our ends." This, of course, was intolerable.

The members of this group were informed that they would not be admitted to the University beginning with the next semester. They wanted to be expelled but neither they nor their sponsors were given that satisfaction.

The time was the hysterical postwar period. She was an attractive co-ed, a dormitory resident. He was a good-looking young man sent to the University by a government bureau to investigate the young lady as a dangerous enemy agent. He entered, with permission, as a student, became acquainted with the suspect, and cultivated the friendship assiduously for several months. Parties, games, and concerts were in order day and night. She had a wonderful time at the expense of the government until, toward the end of the semester, it was discovered that the agent had been sent to the wrong university. He disappeared overnight, I am sure regretfully. She was charming.

Another case of discipline for which I had perforce to take entire responsibility occurred when a famous singer gave a concert in Hill Auditorium.

The lady appeared on the concert stage in a phenomenal gown and a weird hat the like of which had not been seen in Ann Arbor. She created a sensation among the students. The next morning when I came to the office my secretary informed me that the lady was calling me on the telephone. It happened I knew the artist personally, but I could not believe she was calling me because I had been informed she was to leave Ann Arbor shortly after the concert. Unfortunately, she had not departed. When I answered the phone she assured me in broken but vigorous English that she had been very "insult" and wanted "recompense." I tried to soothe her and to discover the cause of her agitation. She informed me in no uncertain terms in three languages.

The *Michigan Daily* had published a review of the concert

in which her clothes were described with some facetiousness, but her singing was unmentioned. She was assured that the editors would be promptly disciplined. I had my secretary call the editors and the drama critic to my office. As they stood before me I explained that the complaint had been made and I intended to discipline them. There was a period of silence and then I remarked, "You are to understand you are disciplined, good morning."

I later wrote the lady a letter informing her that the boys now realized that they had been disciplined. Everyone's honor was satisfied.

I was moved at one time, after an experience in Egypt, to remark to our dean of students that it might be well on some occasions to adopt a disciplinary method of a friend of mine— the sheik of a village near our "dig" at Karanis. I had secured a new car for our staff. As it was being driven from Cairo to the camp some children in the village threw stones at it. Our director complained to the sheik who said he would look into the matter. In a few days he appeared at camp with the information that the incident would not be repeated. When asked what measures had been taken to protect the car on its frequent trips through the village he remarked, "I have whipped the children, but I have whipped the fathers a good deal harder. Parents should know better than to have such children."

It is to be hoped that the advice I was called on to give students from time to time did not often result disastrously. Some of it didn't, I am happy to record.

A student in one of the professional schools came to me in his last year in college to ask about courses in other schools that he might take. Among others he listed "music appreciation." He wasn't exactly clear what this course was about. To find out what he had in mind, I asked him for his major objective. He replied: "Well, you see, Mr. President, I am in a professional school and finding that I have some extra hours this semester I thought I should take at least one crack at culture." I asked him what he thought about Shakespeare and was glad to have him reply that while he had never read Shakespeare he understood he was "quite a guy." He took a course in Shakespeare.

The dean of women was frustrated and appealed to me. The student had requested permission to drive a car. She in no way qualified for the privilege. She insisted her father wanted her to have a car while in school and submitted a letter from him to that effect. Since no reason was given I wrote to the parent. The father answered by telephone. "Yes, I wrote the letter. I couldn't refuse her. For God's sake, don't grant my request."

The relation of the student to his university can never be expressly defined. It will vary with the student and the extent to which the institution accepts responsibility for his training. I have always held the belief that the school should provide for the student informal as well as formal training for life. This was the primary reason that very soon after coming to the campus we started our student teas.

From the beginning we tried to impress the students that these were not special functions. They simply represented the setting aside of a time when the President and his wife would be "at home." It was our intention to keep the teas as informal as any afternoon gathering of the family. At first one or two students came and the numbers increased very slowly. We were careful not to give the impression that the students were neglecting us by not coming to the house. A few months after the teas started I was waited on by some of the men who told me

I was probably disappointed that more students didn't come to see us. They suggested it was because we were using the word "tea," and the students were a little shy of attending these functions, thinking they were probably "stiff" affairs. My reply was that we were not disappointed. We felt the students would come when they learned we wanted to know them but only if they cared to know us. We could not change the name because they would have to encounter such functions later in life, and we thought it advantageous for them to find out, if they didn't know, that there was nothing necessarily stilted about them. They accepted my explanation probably more readily than they would today, when the "tea" with its cheering beverages, cookies, cakes, and intelligent conversation has largely given way to the "cocktail party" with its liquor, decayed fish, canapés, and inane talk.

We made a point to have in the library, in addition to my books, autographed publications of members of the faculty and occasionally we asked faculty men to drop in and give the students a chance to meet them. It did not take more than six or eight months before many students, often two hundred or more on an afternoon, felt quite free to come to the house.

We had many interesting experiences at these teas, some really heart-warming, some amusing.

A young freshman came for his first visit determined to hold his own in conversation. He sought Mrs. Ruthven as soon as he entered and informed her that the doorbell wasn't working very well. She was not to worry about it, however, for he was going to be an engineer and would come over the next week and fix it. I don't know whether he did or not, but the bell did get repaired.

The same students, of course, did not appear each week, but noticing one boy who returned a second and a third consecutive week Mrs. Ruthven told him how pleased we were that he kept coming back. His reply was, "Oh, I had to finish the book I started in the library."

Two young ladies were coming in the door just as I was going through the hall. One of them said, "Mary, you aren't getting along very well in history." Mary admitted it. Her trouble was that she could not concentrate. The comment of the first girl was, "I know it, and I can tell you this, you had better concentrate or you'll find yourself an alumna of ———" (a girls' college I won't mention for fear of reprisals).

A new student from China was brought to one of the teas immediately on his arrival in Ann Arbor by the director of the International Center. I asked the director, who had telephoned beforehand, if the boy could speak English. He assured me that he could. When he came in I said, "Good afternoon, Mr. Chang," whereupon he bowed very politely and said, "Good afternoon, sir or madam as the case may be." This since became, I understand, a favorite story of Lowell Thomas and Bennett Cerf.

Student on observing a series of books labeled *Catalogue of Snakes* in my science library:

"Mr. President, is this the faculty directory?"

In addition to little incidents there were generally very interesting conversations and discussions at the teas. The talk wasn't often about athletics or student politics. One afternoon I walked into my study during a lull in incoming guests and found a group of ten or twelve students sitting in a circle on the floor engaged in intense discussion. Some of the students saw me come in, and I was delighted that they did not interrupt their conversation. One of them reached up his hand and pulled me down into the circle. I soon found that in the group were Catholics, Jews, a Zoroastrian, and representatives of at least two Protestant churches. I shall always insist these students were discussing comparative religion more objectively and with deeper knowledge than one would expect from a group of adults not specially selected.

There are usually to be found in the student body those who talk and write freely about University affairs and educational problems and purport to represent "student opinion." As a matter of fact I learned much more about student reactions to University changes and educational movements from the students at the teas than I did from reading the often ill-considered, half-baked, and biased discussions in the student newspaper.

The advent of war was not allowed to interfere with our "at homes." Of course there were food shortages, but Mrs. Ruthven insisted that as always she was going to do her part to make the students realize someone on the campus other than the military was interested in them. Not only were the teas continued, but she provided as usual only homemade cakes and cookies which she was able to do with the gifts of scarce materials contributed by faculty families.

This seems now to have been a small contribution to the war effort, but it was remarkable how the young people in a troubled period seemed to feel that, at least as far as their campus life was concerned, they were at home in our house.

With the close of World War II, to provide living quarters for married veteran students, the University took over a large section of the housing development that had been constructed for the employees of the bomber plant at Willow Run—eight miles from the campus. The houses were temporary, two-room, coal-stove-heated structures. Living conditions were simple, but the University provided a resident director, a bus service to and from Ann Arbor, and in other ways endeavored to make the students feel that they were an integral part of the University family. The spirit of those students was excellent. The young women organized sewing parties, card parties, dances, and other forms of recreation. The men did above-average academic work. The one certain way to arouse their ire, men or women, was to suggest they were underprivileged. Mrs. Ruthven and I visited with these young families in their recreation center, and on these occasions urged them to call the appropriate offices when in need of University assistance. On one of these visits I added that when they did not know whom to call they should feel free to come to me. In the immediate postwar period there were still many shortages, and I was soon told of one. A group of Willow Run wives called at my office and reminded me of my offer of assistance. Their problem was cloth for diapers for babies, here and in prospect. With the co-operation of the superintendent of the University Hospital, who in my experience had never been stumped by anything, I was able to make good.

In the first days of my regime it seemed about as difficult for students to transfer from one school or college to another as for the proverbial "camel to go through the eye of a needle." There was a tradition that if a student did not get along in one college he could not be accepted directly in another. This would be a reflection on the standards of scholarship proclaimed by the latter. This did not seem to me to make much sense.

It would seem wise to make it easy for a student to transfer from one school or college to another when in the opinion of his instructors it is to his advantage to do so. Every university teacher knows that students make mistakes in the selection of their future careers. Sometimes it is immature judgment which is at fault. Often, however, the error is the result of pressures by parents and other relatives.

Whatever the cause, unless the misplaced student can be transferred to the school indicated by his interests and aptitudes, the consequences can be predicted with some certainty. He will be unhappy in college. He will do mediocre work or fail in his

studies. He will, if he continues in college, become dissatisfied
and second-rate.

I had to struggle with a number of these situations partly,
I believe, because so many students felt free to consult me. In
some cases I was able to persuade parents to loosen the reins or
the students to rebel. In others I was not successful in trying
to convince families that father doesn't necessarily always know
best. When I succeeded I got the same satisfaction that came
when I was able to move a man on the staff from an ineffectual
niche in one department to an opening position in another.

A freshman medical student came to me in considerable
distress. He wished to specialize in this field but he was told,
in the opinion of his instructors he would not "make a physi-
cian." He should therefore leave the school. Being impressed by
his sincerity and with some pressure, I had him admitted to the
arts college and advised him to pursue such medical courses as
were available to students of the college. I heard nothing more
of the man for a number of years when I encountered him at
an alumni meeting in New York City. He reminded me of his
experience, and I asked him what he was doing. I was delighted
to find that he was professor of anatomy in one of the best
medical schools in the country.

The young woman was on the carpet. The dean of women
was exploring a rumor and was reporting the case to me for my
amusement. There was at least a suspicion that Mary, a dormitory resident, had lingered too long the preceding night in a local
beer parlor. She listened respectfully while the dean recited the
evidence.

"My dear, you were in a local beer tavern, were you not?"

"Yes, madam."

"When you came home, you were noisy. Do you think you
were slightly intoxicated?"

"Oh no, madam, but I made a very interesting discovery."

"What did you discover, Mary?"

"I learned I am allergic to beer."

Although somewhat elderly, the visitor had a large history book under her arm and was by her own admission a student. Evidently, also, she was physically handicapped and in distress. She was promptly admitted to the office. With difficulty she negotiated the entrance on two crutches.

As the door closed the visitor walked briskly to a far corner, leaned her crutches against the wall, removed her dark glasses, and returned to the guest chair without a trace of lameness. Seating herself, she appeared to be listening to or for something. Finally, she remarked: "The spirits are talking to me. They are telling me to kill you. I must see if I have my gun with me." Evidently, this was the end.

Deep silence prevailed while she searched through an immense handbag. Was this detached feeling of looking at a scene at the cinema characteristic of those about to be shot, hung, or beheaded? There was no fear, no suspense, only a feeling of curiosity.

But the drama was interrupted. A gun was not to be found. She had, we learned later, left it in her room. The lady was persuaded that shooting the President would not produce the grades she desired or even be adequate revenge for not receiving them. Perhaps it would be better to perforate her dean. The suggestion seemed to please her, and, again very lame, she gathered her crutches, handbag, glasses, and book and departed. I tried to justify my suggestion to her dean by quoting the Scriptures to the effect that a live dog is better than a dead lion. He claimed to be unimpressed.

The new president of one of the numerous student organizations was all enthusiasm and determined to make a record for himself and his society. He had no trouble in thinking up activities, but his ambitions were being thwarted by conditions very common among campus groups—the treasury was as bare as the old dame's cupboard, and available attractions were expensive. After much cogitation, when everything seemed quite hopeless, the young president had an inspiration and promptly rushed to the proper university official. This officer referred him to me.

Our meeting resulted in a conversation which brightened an otherwise dull day: "Mr. President, we want to sponsor a lecture to raise money for our group." This seemed to be a good idea, as lectures constitute an approved method of education. I had to ask him, however, if he could find a lecturer on a subject which would draw an audience large enough to insure expenses. "Sure, Mr. President. We can have a talk on advertising which will pack them in the aisles, mow them down, and empty every movie house in town." I asked him if he wasn't a little optimistic. With great enthusiasm he answered: "Why, Mr. President, we could get Sally Rand who is now giving some talks for an advertising firm. Don't you agree with me that she would wow this community?" The young man was probably right, for Sally was at that time a famous fan dancer. Alas, youth was again to be suppressed by age; with how much reluctance no one will ever know.

The student tea was in full swing. The young people were coming in a steady stream and the hostess had not as yet begun to worry about the cakes holding out. Rather casually I noticed on the walk in front of the house a young couple arguing strenuously and I expected them to appear at the door. Suddenly an attractive young thing came hurrying in and rushed up to me without stopping to remove coat or hat, lay down her books, or powder her nose. She was apparently very angry and did not care who knew it. The explanation came speedily. Hers was the fury of a female scorned. "Mr. President, where can I find a dictionary?" Trying to calm her, I replied, "My dear, why not ask me what you want to know? I am an encyclopedia of all knowledge." She was, however, in a fighting mood and would not be appeased. "Is there such a word as 'noisome' and if so how is it spelled?" "Well, there is a word spelled n-o-i-s-o-m-e." "Isn't there a term spelled n-o-i-s-e-s-o-m-e?" she snapped. Not that I knew of, I told her. However, there were archaic words in the dictionary. We retired to the library. It was encouraging to discover such a thirst for knowledge, but disconcerting to note that the little lady's ire abated not a whit as we turned the pages. I pointed out that there was such a word as "noisome," that it meant poisonous among other things, but that there was no such word as "noisesome" at least in Webster. "I don't care what the dictionary says," she sputtered. "I am sorry I asked for it. I have just had a fight with my boy friend. He called me noisome and I know he meant noisy. I don't mind in the least being called poisonous, but I'll not have any man tell me I am loud. 'Noisome' or 'noisesome' he'll have to apologize or I'll never speak to him again."

The senator was a power in the legislature; also a master in his own home. He informed me that his son was preparing to enter Medical School. Would I talk to him? I would. A few days later the young man called on me. I asked him the routine question: Why had he chosen medicine? He hadn't. Medicine was his father's choice. He wanted to be a pharmacist. Would I talk to his father? I certainly would.

The senator was irate, "If you encourage my son in his foolishness, I will oppose the University's budget request. This is none of your business."

"Senator, this is as much my business as it is yours."

Fate saved the situation. The father was taken to Abraham's bosom, and the son continued his studies. I hope he is a good pharmacist.

I had an unorthodox view of admissions which was shared by a wise and experienced registrar. Almost every year he would bring to me records of students who could not quite qualify for admission on their grades but who in his judgment should be accepted. With my connivance these students were admitted, not officially on probation, but with the understanding that if they were unable to carry the work we would assist them to transfer to schools better able to meet their needs. The results from breaking the rules were quite satisfactory.

I don't know that the registrar and I ever formulated our own standards of excellence for entering students. We did not, however, rely on our intuition. Among the traits we looked for were an "insatiable curiosity," a desire to do a good job, and a goal of some kind.

Every administrator knows that on some occasions it is advisable to ignore the rules. When a student's request of this nature was concerned I occasionally asked him to see Professor B, who knew more ways of sidestepping University regulations than anyone else on the staff.

I have been concerned since my teaching days with the over-emphasis on grades, important as they are, as criteria for admission. In our large and expanding institutions this emphasis seems to increase. As a distinguished psychologist has recently observed: "Our national problem is that we have tended to focus increasingly on encouraging one type of excellence, and a practical measurable action-oriented type of excellence at that. Other types of human excellence exist, particularly those involving character and the inner life and the world of imagination and human sensitivity. They can be measured if necessary to combat the stress on academic performance. They too need encouragement and they can be encouraged by less stress on the purely academic side of life and more stress on the unique styles of educational institutions that most influence such other human qualities."

Generally speaking, from the presidency of Dr. Tappan until the time I entered Michigan the housing of students followed the tradition of the German universities—every man for himself. Soon thereafter a dormitory for women was given by alumni—Helen Newberry—and under the presidency of Dr. Hutchins, Martha Cook was built, also the gift of an alumnus. Betsy Barbour was another house for women, given by an alumnus, and a fourth, Mosher-Jordan Hall, was later erected on a bond issue subscribed by a group of alumni. With these exceptions, students were expected to find accommodations in private homes and boarding houses unless elected to fraternities or sororities.

My immediate predecessor as President and the then dean of students were much concerned with the housing conditions for both men and women, as well they should have been. While the University inspected and listed "approved" rooming houses, some students were forced to live in substandard quarters. The situation was bound to worsen as attendance was increasing. The President and the dean insisted that the University should proceed without delay to plan a program of dormitory construction. This stirred up a hornet's nest in the community.

Retired persons supporting themselves by operating boarding and rooming houses, others augmenting slender incomes by taking in a roomer or two, and even some businessmen joined forces and attacked the President on all fronts—in Ann Arbor, in the legislature, and through the alumni.

It soon became evident after the retirement of Dr. Little that there was no real reason for continuing the fracas. Conditions were changing rapidly. With the expansion of the physical plant the University began to purchase houses in the vicinity of the campus to the profit of the owners of the larger rooming and boarding houses. The trend toward building small homes and apartment houses was proceeding rapidly.

While I escaped the controversy when I came into office I was faced with an increasingly serious problem of student housing. It was evident that the University would have to accept more responsibility in this area. I hoped that a dormitory program, when adopted, would provide more than rooms and board —that the houses would be centers of informal education and cultural growth.

As one observer of the social scene puts it: "There are other types of human excellence [than academic performance] without which life would hardly be worth living, and I do not mean sewing or the art of polite conversation. I do mean such characteristics as sensitivity to other human beings, compassion, richness and variety of imaginative life, or a lifelong concern for a particular scientific problem whether one is paid to work on it or not. These are less visible and less measurable types of human excellence, but nevertheless important for all that."

In short, the houses should offer students some of the advantages provided by the English colleges and claimed, often erroneously, to be inherent in fraternity living. This in general was the objective of the Michigan House Plan.

Those concerned with the development of a dormitory system were convinced that the most immediate need was improved housing for freshmen. The first year of college is a period of environmental conditioning and often very difficult. Group living can facilitate an adjustment.

The basic problem was, of course, financial. I discussed the situation with an old friend, the president of the Ann Arbor Trust Company. He suggested studying the possibility of financing dormitories on a self-liquidating basis. The first question was whether, taking into consideration costs of construction and reasonable charges for board and room, bonds could be issued that would bear reasonable maturities. He reported that this was apparently quite possible. The second question could only be answered through experience: Even though the bonds would be tax free, would they still be attractive to investors if they were secured only by confidence in the Board of Regents? It did not seem to me that other support for a loan of this kind should be necessary, certainly not a mortgage or a pledge of student fees (tuition).

At a meeting of the Board of Regents held in Lansing I proposed that we erect a dormitory for first-year men by this method. After considerable hesitation and with one abstention, they voted to try the experiment. At the close of the meeting as we were leaving the room one of the Board members remarked: "If the plan is a good one why not start with two buildings? One will not materially ease the situation." I reconvened the meeting and received approval to proceed with the construction of the first two houses for men—Allen and Rumsey, later combined into one unit.

The bonds proved acceptable to investors, and following construction of Allen House and Rumsey House, the University built the West Quadrangle, the East Quadrangle, the South Quadrangle, and Victor Vaughan House for men, took over the bonds on Mosher-Jordan Hall, and constructed additional houses for women.

It was unfortunate that in building the so-called South Quadrangle it was necessary, because of the pressing need for rooms and the costs of construction, to depart from the general plan of the East and West Quadrangles. The arrangement of the houses in the South Quadrangle only partly succeeds in making the building much different from a hotel.

The educational features of the Michigan House Plan were developing satisfactorily in the East and West Quadrangles in the first years of their operation. However, World War II, the postwar influx of veterans, and, later, the continuing increase in the number of students destroyed most of the cultural advantages. The name continued in use, but came to apply principally to the mechanics of operation.

I never attempted, as I have said, to define the extent to which the University should stand *in loco parentis* to the students. There are too many variables to be considered. Manners and customs and even standards of taste vary almost from year to year. The students at Michigan, as in other schools, vary individually in habitudes, aptitudes, and social backgrounds and thus in their reactions to college life. At various times the college student has been labeled lazy, hard-working, serious, frivolous, radical, liberal, conservative, according to the prejudices of the uninformed. He is, of course, none of these things and at the same time all of them.

While a type student description is impossible to formulate, the experienced teacher can recognize certain groups. Based on adjustment to the college environment three categories have always interested me.

The noisy ones: From the time they enter college they are determined to be heard. Posing as authorities on almost everything at home and abroad, they insist they should run the University. They are so vociferous that they sometimes annoy the public, the alumni, and the legislature. They usually claim to be liberals and boast of disrespect for authority. Common status symbols are, according to the mode, soiled shoes, jeans, shorts, untidy hair, and occasionally mangy beards. These students should disturb no one. One can usually assume that their activities represent growing pains. My disappointment with them as I have seen them later as alumni is that very few become liberal leaders and many become distressingly ultraconservative.

He had a wonderful life as a student. He had on more than one occasion criticized the President, insulted the deans, and even questioned the authority of the Regents. A day or two before Commencement he called on the President's secretary.

"Miss R., I have been an aggravation to the President, but I am going to make him proud of me."

"George, he hasn't complained. But do your best."

Three years later he called on me, was invited to lunch, and was asked about his career. He was a personnel officer in a large industrial concern noted for its labor troubles. He had helped execute a union contract much to the advantage of his company. In general, in his opinion, requests for fringe benefits were an unjustified device of union officials to keep themselves in office. As he was leaving, he remarked:

"Dr. Ruthven, I told your secretary when I left college I would someday make you proud of me. How have I done?"

"George, for the first time, I am not proud of you."

The playboys (and girls): Much has been said and written about the young people who go to college only on the insistence of their parents or because it is "the thing to do." Complaints are often heard about the waste of money and the time of instruction in trying to educate those whose ambition is to get nothing more than a "gentleman's grade" or to get married. In my experience this group has always been a small one at Michigan. The critics fail to take into consideration the number of these students who find themselves after they have entered college and go on to success as alumni and citizens.

The dedicated ones: The students who more than any others make life worth living for their teachers are those who come to college with their eyes firmly fixed on at least a general goal. They refuse to be discouraged by adversity or diverted from their course by the college sideshows. Once called "grinds" by the playboys and considered poor college citizens by the noisy ones these men and women have in later years gained the more respectable title of "eggheads." Neither of these terms is appropriate.

The young man had one liability. He was broke. His assets were a determination to be a doctor, a good mind, and some facility as a boxer. He came to Michigan determined to earn his expenses in the prize ring and became a professional for that purpose. He never lost sight of his major objective, however, and his instructors encouraged him by attending all of his bouts. When he entered Medical School after his college work he was told to stop his pugilistic career because he might ruin his hands. Again, he was not discouraged. He completed his ten years of professional training and is now chief of his service in one of the most famous hospitals in the United States.

THE FACULTY

Having in effect grown up with them I had, when I became the University's chief executive, many friends and many more acquaintances on the staff. While it may sometimes have appeared otherwise, to my knowledge none of my former colleagues ever attempted to take advantage of our friendship. Indeed, I noted that many of those with whom I had been previously most closely associated even took pains to avoid giving the appearance of doing so.

My most pleasant memories now are the recollections of the understanding, encouragement, advice, and active assistance I received from my associates in good times and bad.

Early in my years as an instructor I overheard a remark by a dean of the Graduate School which I never forgot. He was discussing the allocation of research funds and the criteria to be considered in recommending promotions of staff members. It was his observation that the persons most heard on the campus were often those least heard of abroad. I interpreted this as an excuse to avoid committee assignments and faculty and Senate meetings, thus getting more time for my studies. I later came to see that the intimation that faculty men should talk less and do more about research could be taken too literally.

When I was asked to become the dean of administration I explained how I had organized my life to avoid interference with my studies, hoping to get the sympathy of the President, himself a biologist. This appeal was not effective. His response was, "Don't you think you have had more than your share of fun and should now help carry the load of general administration?"

It is fortunate that there are faculty members who enjoy participating in university affairs. As President I never thought these men should be penalized for doing little or no creative work. To be sure it seems sometimes that of the making of many committees there is no end, and many committee meetings are a weariness of the flesh. At the same time many university chores can be much better done by boards and temporary and permanent committees than by executives. In this kind of business the researcher is inclined to take little interest, I confess, not always to his credit.

A few years before I retired I made a discovery about university teachers which surprised me. As every college man knows students have ways of rating instructors. They are said to require more or less work, to mark low or high, to be strict or lax about class attendance, and in general to be easy-going or tough. In visiting with alumni it gradually dawned on me that with the passing of the years memories of the "popular" professors tended to become dim—often even their names could not be recalled. On the other hand the hard taskmasters—even those who were said to be "hated" by the students—were often remembered not in resentment but in sincere appreciation.

Academic freedom has been so much discussed and written about that there would seem to be little more that needs to be said on the subject. Even in these "enlightened times," however, a university president may receive demands to muzzle an instructor for his alleged heretical or subversive views. On occasion a young learner will be slow to accept new ideas and will give wrong interpretations of the teachings of his instructor. A teacher may sometimes, in his enthusiasm, appear as a crusader rather than an educator. Parents, alumni, churchmen, narrow-minded businessmen, and others now and then ignore and even resent the continuing increase in the body of knowledge and question the obligation and freedom of the teacher to teach and the student to learn.

On very few occasions did I consider it necessary to bring to a faculty member a criticism of his "advanced thinking." The task of dealing with the critics on the other hand was often time-consuming and not seldom a delicate one.

When controversial subjects were in the field of the natural sciences I could usually reduce the heat. I really enjoyed quietly pointing out that professors could not burn the books of Malthus, Darwin, Mendel, modern geneticists, and other biologists. Neither could they ignore biological principles and the facts of paleontology, archeology, anthropology, or any other of the natural sciences.

I can say now that in other sensitive fields I had four valuable consultants: a Catholic priest, a Methodist minister, a Jewish rabbi, and a philosopher. These scholars refused to believe that God selected the children to be born with twelve fingers instead of ten and the adults who in their old age were to enjoy the sweet uses of adversity, and that this is the best of possible worlds.

During my undergraduate years, as I have said, it was the discoveries of the biologists which caused the most violent controversies and endangered the positions of many teachers. The conflict was largely inspired by the clergy and principally affected the public schools and church colleges. This era in the history of biology all but came to an end in the Scopes trial and the ridiculous debates between Bryan and Darrow.

This was not the case in other fields. Even when I was President I received suggestions from churchmen that certain professors be muzzled for teaching heretical doctrines, and I occasionally suggested to teachers that they might be more tactful and patient, but never that they should become hypocritical.

As a graduate student I discovered in a genus of snakes a method of variation which I thought would be of assistance to taxonomists in determining the relationships of species in other genera. To confirm some of my findings I spent several weeks studying materials in the United States National Museum. I was pleased when the distinguished chief of the division of reptiles and amphibians agreed with my conclusions, but I was depressed when a short time afterward in a published paper he ignored my contribution to science. He explained when reproached: "Ruthven, I agree with your findings but remember you young scientists must be patient. You cannot expect general acceptance of your discoveries until some of the older generation dies off and we die hard." This lesson I took to heart.

In short, my method of dealing with criticisms of the faculty was to avoid public arguments and patiently to explore the facts in private conversations, thus permitting the critics to save face.

A serious threat to academic freedom appeared after World War II as the result of communistic propaganda. This philosophy, involving as it does many fields of instruction, has made an impact on high schools and colleges and universities both public and private. Being contrary to the so-called "American way of life" it quickly disturbed many persons and became attractive to crackpots and the underprivileged.

My position was simply and consistently that qualified teachers disposed to teach their subjects objectively should be free to do so. Students have the right to hear both sides of controversial questions. At the same time teachers do not have a right to abuse these privileges by resorting to propaganda, nor may students interfere with the operations of the universities. In acting on this belief in the crises which arose I found myself to my amusement classed as a conservative by the extreme liberals and as at least a "pink" by the witch hunters.

Academic freedom will never be fully achieved—humans

being what they are—but the fight to achieve it must continue to be waged by administrators as well as by teachers, regardless of cost. Occasional skirmishes will be lost, but pacifism in this struggle will only impede the war effort and will gain the respect of no one.

The professor had aroused the ire of the politicians. He was promoting a change in the machinery of government which would be a serious blow to that sacred cow—patronage. "He was involving the University in politics." "He should be muzzled or fired."

The budget requests to the legislature had been held up until near the close of the session. The University did not reply to the criticisms. Finally, I was called before the Ways and Means Committee. The chairman greeted me: "Mr. President, we have reviewed your requests and found them satisfactory. We want to know, however, if we approve your budget, what you are going to do with Professor Jim."

"Mr. Chairman, I intend to increase his salary."

When the laughter subsided the chairman said, "Dr. Ruthven, we thought you would say that, and we are glad you did. Don't let the legislature run the University."

As a teacher I believed that changes in educational procedures should be left to the faculties. I saw no reason to change this opinion after I became President. One of the troubles of my predecessor resulted from his attempts to put a program into effect which needed careful study by those who would have to implement it. Essentially, the plan had merit. My method was always to make and to take suggestions on educational reforms and then work with the deans and committees to put them into effect. I am sure that I overworked the word co-operation, but I hope it was never true as one disgruntled professor remarked:

"The President believes in co-operation, he to do the operating, we to do the co-ing."

Up to and including my years as a teacher, research, while not discouraged, was not encouraged at Michigan. To be sure, the professor was respected who could, with a full-time teaching load, find time for original studies, but funds for the purpose were meager. The feeling seemed to prevail that legislative appropriations were to be used solely for teaching purposes. At any rate the need for research facilities should not appear as an item in budget requests to the legislature.

For years I was told also that the Regents had a rule that no publications were to be issued by the University with the exception of official bulletins of information. Despite staff impressions that the support of original studies was not a proper use of state funds, ambitious scholars found time for research. Some needed funds were extracted from departmental budgets, and some were received as gifts from private sources and as grants from foundations. I insisted research was not an avocation of professors but a responsibility and a function of universities— public and private.

In the general encouragement of original investigations I encountered little opposition either from the legislature or the Regents.

I was assisted in my determination to promote original investigations by a discovery made while preparing my first budget as dean of administration. For years the management of the University had been too largely in the hands of the Business Office. Each year the President would be informed of the amount available for budget purposes, and this sum was always little more than was needed to cover the costs of instruction and plant maintenance. At the same time it was customary for the Business Office to maintain very large reserves which did not appear as contingency items. I insisted that only a small contingency fund was needed, that the appropriations should be used each year; that research should be considered an important part of the academic program, and that while legal it was not honest to accumulate or to use reserves from operating funds for plant expansion.

To the time of my retirement the feeling seemed to exist on the campus that the support of certain types of scholarly investigations, such as field studies in foreign lands, was not a legitimate expenditure. I could not agree to such a limitation of university activities. If objectives of research are the increase of knowledge and the encouragement of teachers, studies which contribute to these objectives are as legitimate in a state school as in a private one. Surely in a university, as distinguished from a trade school, such studies as the gestation period of the wallaby, the habits of a Brazilian ant, the significance of the Dead Sea Scrolls, or the excavation of a buried city in the Near East are of no less value than investigations into the qualities of plastics, the number of calories in breakfast foods, or the effectiveness of a brand of tooth paste.

Paradoxical as it may seem, many universities today have both too little and too much financial support for "research." As in the past, few if any of them have sufficient funds to permit full use of the talents of their faculties in the fields of pure, basic, or fundamental research. At the same time, enormous sums of money are being poured into schools for "research" which should more appropriately be designated as developmental, technological, or contractual investigation.

Few will disagree that the university provides a favorable environment for basic research. Through the years, this has been amply demonstrated. In the atmosphere of the campus the professors find encouragement for intellectual growth, freedom to attack the boundaries of knowledge in their special fields, and opportunities to rear new generations of scholars.

There are many observers, and I am one, who feel that contractual investigations should have a very small place in the program of an institution of higher learning. Admittedly, opportunities to obtain generous—sometimes fantastic—sums for this type of work are enticing to professors, especially to those not interested in basic investigations, particularly if increased stipends and freedom from teaching are entailed. The chance is looked upon favorably by some administrators as a means of increasing the prestige of their institution, especially if the overhead provisions in the contracts are large enough or—preferably —a little larger than the incidental costs.

Difficulties encountered in fulfilling research contracts, I discovered, appear soon after they are accepted:

university administrative costs are increased;

professors are taken away from their regular responsibilities;

new men, often of less than university caliber, frequently have to be engaged for the projects;

perplexing problems of salary, tenure, titles, and fringe benefits are created;

the graduate students, who are often employed, are used mostly as technical assistants and have little or no opportunity for independent growth; and

two university castes are formed, the scholars and the technologists, with an underlying feeling of mutual disrespect.

If honest confession is good for the soul, I should feel better when I admit, as I now do, that I was slow in reaching the conclusion that the laboratories of technical schools, industry, and government are the proper environment for developmental investigations.

An academic freedom which should not be sacrificed is the freedom of the faculty member to engage in freewheeling research in any field of interest to him.

As director of the Museum and later as President, I was never able to find any basis for the impression prevalent when I was an instructor that the Regents were opposed to publication at University expense of scholarly papers and books. They had authorized the Humanistic Series, and they did not object when I initiated several Museum series. These were at first privately financed, but later, with others, were supported by the University. Furthermore, no objection was raised to the purchase by the Museum of reprints—those valuable tools of the investigator.

As every scholar realizes, it is to the advantage of a university to maintain a press. Scholarly work becomes of full value only as it appears in print, and in many fields the opportunities for publication are limited. My view has been that liberal financial support of a press, like the cost of research, should be considered legitimate university expense. A university press which is compelled to operate as a moneymaking department even to the extent of being self-supporting should be given some other name than "university."

Among the improvements and expansions in our educational programs, several which presented opportunities for research were especially interesting to me. For these I had strong faculty support. They included the worker-education project wrecked by the man who was later to associate workers with bird dogs, the initiation of studies in human genetics (with no encouragement from the Medical School), the Institute of Human Adjustment, the Michigan Historical Collections, the School of Social Work, the Museum of Classical Archeology (later the Kelsey Museum), and the splendid growth of the Extension Division. These developments gave increased facilities for teaching and research.

Throughout my college days I often heard state universities referred to as "Godless institutions." When I accepted my first appointment in the University one of my college professors said facetiously he thought I was in less danger than students who went on to other state schools in that Michigan had an "Angell" for a president. It was a bad pun but reflected the thinking in church schools.

In my earlier years at Michigan students had little opportunity for developing an interest in the field of religion and an opinion prevailed that state schools were proscribed from "teaching religion." There were a few courses on the campus such as The Bible as Literature and some courses in comparative religion. The students had an independent organization known as the Student Christian Association, a voluntary activity, and the local churches supported student guilds. These were inadequate for the students who wished to pursue intensive studies of the religious backgrounds of different faiths.

I was able in the course of time, with the aid of a religious counselor, to change the Student Christian Association into a Student Religious Association and to introduce some programs in the field which a student could elect. I argued with my colleagues in charge of public-supported institutions in other states that the phrase often used in public education, "the teaching of religion," really meant in the minds of the originators of the system the teaching of sectarianism.

I was not brought up in what conventionally would be known as a religious family, but while I was in college I was fortunate enough to take, in addition to my other work, courses in the Bible, Christian Evidences, and Natural Theology. There developed from this early introduction to the field an interest in comparative religion which with my work in science has been instrumental in forming my concept of the nature of the world and man.

I hoped that through our student religious center and programs in religious studies the wide variety of faiths represented in the student body could come together with opportunities for discussions and mutual understanding and respect. The process was slow, but in later years for those students who took advantage of the cultural opportunities presented in and about the center the hope materialized. It seems wrong for a University which purports to offer broad opportunities for the training of students for good citizenship to ignore an area of thought that has so greatly affected the consciences, ideals, and aspirations of mankind.

As a new President I had reason, as I have said, to be grateful to the faculty. Older members helped me to learn quickly the traditions and practices of the schools and colleges, generously responding to my frequent requests for advice and constructive criticism. However, except for the complete extroverts, the lives of college presidents are lonely. One satisfaction I experienced and have expressed many times was the feeling that I had been placed by the faculty only on a small hill, not isolated on a mountain top. On one occasion I was told, when a group of professors from several universities were discussing their problems that one of our men remarked: "At Michigan our president is at heart a member of his faculty." It was an accolade I tried hard to merit.

As an instructor I occasionally had harsh words to say about the "administration." This is the privilege of staff members, as it is the prerogative of students to complain of dormitory food. While I expected to hear, now and then, disapprobation of an administrative decision from members of the faculty, I felt sure there would be some objections that would not come to my ears. Only when I learned of disapproval of university policies and practices which were based on unfounded rumor and gossip did I attempt explanations, sometimes with curious results.

A professor had made some witty but serious charges against the Buildings and Grounds Department in a dinner party conversation. When the disturbing news was brought to me I invited the critic to my office. I told him I knew he would be glad to know that the "facts" he cited were incorrect. For a few minutes there was silence, and then came the comment: "Mr. President, I am surprised that anyone pays any attention to what I say at a dinner party."

He was a good teacher—also cantankerous, likable, naive, and voluble. He enjoyed nothing better than to criticize the administration and his colleagues in Senate meetings. It was his idea that no Senate or faculty meeting was successful without a violent argument. Although often careless with facts and sometimes even personally abusive to his associates, they tolerated him. I usually had to refrain from answering his criticisms, for otherwise nothing would be done. After a meeting when he had been frustrated in his attempts to start a controversy, he came to my office.

"Mr. President, you know I have nothing against you or your administration, but I want you to know that our faculty is a herd of sheep. They should fight, fight, fight."

"Well, Mr. K., what should they fight?"

"Why, everything. Did you notice in the last three meetings when I tried to start something, someone moved to adjourn?"

"But, Mr. K., it was nearly six o'clock when you rose to speak and getting near to the dinner hour."

"That's it, that's just it. They are afraid of their wives."

As an executive I quickly learned a lesson later read for me by a one-time professor at Michigan, who became a distinguished scholar. Everything he didn't like was the fault of the "administration," and he disliked almost everything. After a few years he was called to another institution and after a time was made a dean. He soon resigned the position.

Years later we were sitting together on a platform listening to speeches and equally bored. He leaned over and whispered:

"I regret my critical attitude at Michigan."

"Oh, well, Professor Smith, any executive probably needs the goad now and then."

"At the same time, Mr. President, I believe it would be good for his soul if every professor would be made to serve some time as an administrator." I agreed.

Despite the hysteria of the postwar years I had but once to ask for the resignation of professors who were avowed communists. We had little concern for the political leanings of the two men, but objected to their activities. Like the students mentioned elsewhere they chose to advertise themselves by refusing to co-operate in any way with colleagues in their department and college. I had to tell them that I objected to men trying to achieve martyrdom on false issues.

It is an old cliché that a university is its faculty. I prefer the proverb attributed to Caxton: "The walles maken not the strong castellee but the defense of good folke maketh hit empregnable."

At times I was asked to serve as judge in differences of opinion between faculty members. Some cases were difficult to adjudicate.

The old customs and plain speaking were good enough for the retired dean, a rugged individualist, proud of his pioneer upbringing. His quarrel was with the editor of scholarly publications, a purist and a stickler for the use of "dignified" words. He was hard of hearing. The men were good friends, but had fallen out over the use of a word the dean insisted on using in a book he was publishing and the editor was editing.

The editor arrived first.

"Mr. President, I am very much disturbed. The old doctor is a close friend, but he insists on using an archaic and unpleasant word in describing the food of the American Indians."

When the dean entered the office he shouted: "What's

wrong with the word 'vittles'? Mac is a scholar and a good friend but he objects to 'vittles.' He won't listen to me. You know, Mr. President, he is deaf and I can't tell when he can't hear me and when he doesn't want to. We've decided to accept your decision."

The results of the conference can be found in the dean's book.

GIFTS

As a university official both before and after I became President I refused personal gifts except for a few minor ones from close friends. I had but one experience, as director of the University Museums, with the vicuna coat, deep-freeze, and tractor variety of present that might be interpreted as a bribe.

It was my responsibility to plan and supervise the construction of the new University Museums building. The architects asked me to visit two large steel-fabricating companies in Pittsburgh to discuss various details before awarding the contracts. In the discussions with one company I discovered it was being delicately suggested that if this firm received the contract I could expect to find in my bank account $10,000. "No questions will be asked. It is simply a routine business matter. No, it is not possible to deduct the amount from the contract." The proposal was shocking to a college professor who had at least been taught the meaning of intellectual honesty.

I have sometimes felt that I went farther than necessary in declining personal gifts. One offer I frequently recall.

The sheik was a good friend of our archeologists in the Fayoum. With his four wives and children he resided in a village in the oasis. At a dinner which he gave in my honor he learned of my interest in horses. A few days later he and his brother, beautifully attired, galloped into our camp on two magnificent Arab stallions. Dismounting, the sheik offered me my choice. No horse-loving president of a university should be so tempted.

It has always been my thought that the president of a state-supported school should not be expected to solicit private gifts. He will, of course, encourage voluntary support and assist in obtaining grants from foundations for special purposes. Otherwise, he should be busy enough with his executive responsibilities. Personal appeals for funds should be made by the Regents or a university-relations officer. I hope this unorthodox opinion is more than a rationalization of a deep-seated aversion to asking people for money. Only twice, as I now recall, was it necessary for me to make a personal appeal for private contributions.

People of means are popularly supposed to be game on which there is no closed season. The "money birds" are depicted by the "comics" as constantly on the alert to avoid being bagged and college presidents as more or less skillful trackers who are quite willing to fire at their prey either sitting or on the wing. Support is given to this concept of the relation between the college and its potential patrons by the practices of some college administrators.

I soon learned that there are presidents who through choice, the insistence of trustees, or the poverty of their schools spend most of their time in the jungles of the business world in search of a weak or unsuspecting millionaire. These hunters shoot on sight, sometimes by a lucky shot bringing down the meat, but often only crippling their victims and coming home with a "hand-out" and ill-will toward the college.

This picture, true in some particulars, on the whole creates a degrading image of one of our most important institutions. It also does injustice both to presidents as a group and to many public-spirited citizens. Most patrons of schools sincerely consider themselves as stewards of their wealth, at least now and then, and have some understanding of the objectives and needs of institutions of higher learning. They are not only willing but anxious to work with administrative officers and staff members.

The claim that the conditions attached to gifts are necessarily "strings" which hamper their best use is erroneous. To be sure, donors vary in their interests, but it is unfair to assume that these interests are usually selfish. I came to recognize four major groups of benefactors: those who desire to erect buildings, those who prefer to support specific activities, those who desire that gifts bear their names, and those who insist upon remaining anonymous. There are some advantages to the institution and to individual donors in recognizing these differences.

Granting that a college should strive for well-rounded development, certain conclusions seemed obvious. Buildings and equipment are as important as any other facilities in teaching and research. When a gift bears the name of the giver it stimulates others. Some donors must hide their light under a bushel to keep it from being smothered by cranks with a mission and grafters with a racket. Under ideal conditions patrons and executives will work together to make gifts of genuine use to the college and a source of satisfaction both to the giver and to the receiver. A gift made reluctantly or diverted from its original purpose after it is received does nothing to improve the reputation of the recipient.

It may be an idealistic view but in my opinion the wise president will insist on being more than a fund raiser in the ordinary sense. He will put his talents and those of his staff to work to make his institution worthy of support and as good as he thinks or says it is. Prospective donors should have good reasons to consider it a privilege to part with their money in support of higher education. Trustees of state schools should be active in securing financial support and not view contributions as dependent on the persuasive powers of the chief executive. Public-spirited benefactors—generally wise in the ways of the world— are not inclined to try to save a hopelessly wrecked ship, to pour money down rat-holes, or to buy a pig in a poke. When a school or department meets its responsibilities, donors can be expected to be the kind of givers the Lord is said to love.

Some of my experiences illustrate my reasoning in the field of private support and also some of the characteristics of patrons.

My first experience as a fund raiser occurred shortly after I had been made curator of the Museum. My predecessor had secured some financial support from a retired and wealthy lumberman for a small field study by his students. After I came to office I wrote to this prospective donor and asked him if he would be interested in giving some assistance to students in a similar project. The amount involved was small. In due course I received a check in a letter which went on at some length to explain to a young instructor that the writer had earned his money by hard work and did not feel obligated to support the state in its activities. From the tone of his letter I was almost inclined to feel sorry for the gentleman. It happened shortly afterward that I met our professor of forestry on the campus and told him about this letter. He soon contributed to my education. "Ruthven," he said, "don't feel sorry for him. His conscience is hurting him but not enough. He acquired his wealth by leasing the timber rights in a township near Lake Huron. His crews lost their way and when he ended lumbering operations years afterward they found themselves in sight of the shores of Lake Michigan."

I had broken my leg in a very unromantic way. On a cold and slippery winter afternoon I decided to see if I could stay on an ambitious horse. Before starting for the country I had to feed the canine member of the family so that he wouldn't grieve too much in my absence. A slip on an icy porch, a fall, and I found myself in a hospital bed surrounded by doctors, nurses, and interns with carts filled with pipes, ropes, pulleys, and weights.

Several weeks after I had become more or less accustomed to being trussed up like a fowl prepared for the oven, I was told that I was to have an important visitor,—a friend and a potential donor. My nurse, a pulchritudinous and bright girl, suggested setting the stage. Before admitting the caller she carefully arranged the bedclothes so as to expose the ropes, pulleys, and weights and laid out an array of hypodermic syringes, saws, scalpels, and other formidable-looking instruments, including a pair of placental forceps. It was a shocking spectacle to one not familiar with surgical tools.

The visitor, a prosperous automobile executive, arrived all cheerfulness and light. Evidently he was determined his good deed for the day would be to "pick up" the President. He tried one subject of conversation after another but did not carry on very well. He was unable to keep his eyes from the machinery, and seemed to feel that nothing he could say could ease the suffering of a man on the rack. The young "Nightingale" did not help him to any appreciable extent. Gravely and silently she moved about the room occasionally wiping imaginary drops from my brow. Finally, the caller made the supreme effort. Could the University use what was really a handsome gift? Did I have a pet project that needed support? If so, he would like to finance it. The time being up, the gift was promptly accepted and the caller was assisted into his coat by the nurse. After the door had closed it opened again to admit the head of the donor. "Old man," he remarked with a twinkle in his eye, "I'll never know whether I made this gift because of my interest in my University or because I felt so damned sorry for you." The door closed a second time, and the angel of mercy grinned and whispered, "They also serve who only stand and wait—and put on a good act."

One of the most aggravating experiences I had in the general field of alumni giving came to me during Michigan's great Phoenix campaign for funds to support research in the peacetime uses of atomic energy. One of our alumni, a vociferous advocate of free enterprise, had achieved great financial success.

The University in recognition of his success had crowned his achievements with an honorary degree. When the campaign was being organized we expected that since this was an independent project and one of the first efforts to cultivate a new field with enormous possibilities for human welfare it would receive his enthusiastic support. He left us in no doubt. He would have nothing to do with the enterprise. It was a project for the federal government. While many persons of moderate means came to the support of the program he refused to make any contribution. Our conclusion was that in his opinion free enterprise only meant freedom for him to do anything he wanted to do without government interference. I have never forgiven him.

I knew him well. Several times a millionaire and an avowed Christian, his favorite boast was that he was just the steward of his wealth. He did not believe in the PWA, the WPA, or any other form of relief for distressed adults. He was an uncompromising Calvinist. To him failure to provide for old age is clear evidence that the individual is predestined to live his declining years in poverty.

If I knew of a promising young man who needed aid to continue college I must be sure and let him know. I knew such a student and sent him to the "steward." After a rigid examination he was generously offered a loan for a year at 6 per cent interest payable semiannually. "These young men must learn the value of money."

Even a biologist familiar with the law of the survival of the fittest could not like this man.

Another would-be donor has always been an enigma to me. He has long been a close friend and is a generous supporter of philanthropic enterprises, but he has always flatly refused to accept any suggestions, with the result that the University has not had any considerable assistance from him. He evidently thinks he knows the University's needs but cannot decide which ones to support.

Most institutions are offered funds from time to time which they cannot or should not accept. I have had to refuse offers of gifts for the support of researches which stipulated that the results would be the private property of the donor. In my opinion, the results of investigations by a public institution should be made generally available as soon as possible. On one occasion I had to refuse a handsome offer for support of a study of a food product with the understanding that if the findings were unfavorable the company would suppress them; if favorable they would be advertised as the result of company-supported research by University scientists.

On one occasion I did not have a chance to refuse a gift which was in the nature of a bribe. The dean of the Medical School was offered not a few thousands of dollars to accept an unqualified student. The dean declined the offer (he said) without even giving me a chance to refuse a "split."

Unexpected gifts and bequests were always pleasing, particularly when they represented a human interest story involving the University.

When I took office as President I found on my desk among bits of unfinished business a copy of a proposed will leaving the estate of a woman in a distant city for the assistance of students. On inquiry I found that the would-be donor had only been in Ann Arbor for a few hours many years ago. Since that time, about once each year, she had had her attorney draw her will and submit it to the University for approval. Each time the copy was received the Regents found it impossible to approve of the restrictions as to the use of the fund.

The lady was a segregationist in many different directions. She had strong prejudices as to race, creed, color, and nation-

ality. During the years she had been in touch with the University
many letters had been exchanged to no avail. At least one President, the secretary of the University, and the University's attorney had visited her to explain why the institution could not
accept her terms. In discussing with my associates the draft of
the will, our vice-president in charge of business offered to make
another trip to see once again if anything could be done to
liberalize the restrictions. I suggested we make a new start and
propose that the estate be transferred immediately to the University subject to a life-interest in the income. The lady promptly
agreed to receive our representative and stipulated that the meeting take place in the rotunda of the nation's Capitol. A very
brief conference was held. She accepted our suggestion and
within a few days the estate was transferred to the University
with no restrictions except for the life-interest reserved to her.

I was curious to know what prompted the donor's insistence
that the University receive the estate. In reviewing the past correspondence I found the explanation. It seems that in order to
pass the time when she was stranded in Ann Arbor between
trains, she had gone to the campus, where she had asked a young
man which building was the library. He showed her the building
and then, as she tells the story, said, "Madam, you are evidently
a stranger at the University. I have the forenoon free and if you
would like to have me I will spend the morning with you and
show you as much of the University as I can." She concluded in
one letter, "If the University of Michigan has students of this
kind, I am determined it shall have my estate." This episode
might profitably be brought to the attention of each generation
of freshmen.

Another woman whom I never met also deserves an accolade from the University. Although she had lived near the campus for years and was well-known by sight to more than one
generation of Michigan women, few knew her. She was com-
monly thought to be simply a poor, slightly eccentric, modest

old lady. The girls greeted her kindly in the hours she spent in their building contentedly watching her young sisters as they went about their affairs.

At her death it was discovered that she was a retired school teacher with one ambition—to save every penny she could from the income of a small estate in order to leave a bequest for the education of poor girls. For years she had denied herself, and to make sure that her interment would be at a minimum cost to her estate she wished to be buried in her nightclothes in a plain coffin and with no funeral services. As a result of her sacrifices she bequeathed to the University a relatively substantial fund for the purpose dear to her heart.

Some of her requests were not fulfilled. Mrs. Ruthven supplied a dress and through the co-operation of several individuals a respectable coffin was provided. We also held a brief service, and the University counselor in religious education accompanied the body to the family lot in a distant city.

Although she had no direct heirs and had been shamefully neglected by her distant relatives, the lady had scarcely been laid to rest when these relatives attacked her will. After several refusals they found a lawyer to take their case. Finally, unable to secure a compromise they brought suit, a trial was held, and they lost. This was as it should have been, but the suit was nevertheless relatively costly. When the estate came into the hands of the University it was somewhat depleted. It still irritates me that by just the amount spent on court costs are the young women of future generations deprived of educational opportunities.

Every college president can recite similar experiences. Bequests to universities provide manna for some lawyers, and the larger the sum involved the more certain it is to cause trouble and to attract the interest of even "successful" lawyers. Evidently, equities are often ignored by some of the profession.

One of the best-known legal lights of his time, and in his

day a conspicuous figure in national politics, once told our business manager when asked how much he thought a doubtful heir, for whom he was battling, should have: "My dear fellow, you do not understand. The question at issue is not how much the heir should have but how much the lawyers expect to get for themselves." For my comments I might have been sued for libel.

The University has been fortunate in having among its alumni and in its employ lawyers interested in carrying out the wishes of testators. I had, however, to learn in this connection two of the facts of life the hard way. It seems there are few wills which cannot be broken by hook or crook. Directly in proportion to the amount involved is the probability that bequests will be attacked either by greedy or would-be heirs, by hungry barristers, or both.

When wills are written without consultation with college authorities there is great danger that conditions will be laid down which will be not only difficult to follow, but may provide opportunities for legal snarls. On learning this I tried to advise prospective donors to make gifts during their lifetime even though it was necessary to retain a life-interest in the income. There is another reason for urging that benefactions be made before the giver goes to his reward. The objectives of gifts represent, it may be assumed, an interest of the giver. This being true, he should not deprive himself of the satisfaction of seeing his wishes carried out.

When this subject comes to mind I recall the poem of Oliver Wendell Holmes:

> Learn to give
> Money to colleges while you live.
> Don't be silly and think you'll try
> To bother the colleges, when you die,
> With codicil this, and codicil that,

That Knowledge may starve while Law grows fat;
For there never was pitcher that wouldn't spill,
And there's always a flaw in a donkey's will.

The University has the responsibility of being true to the trusts which it accepts. The President and the Regents should try to determine the motive or motives that have inspired the gifts. Only once to my knowledge has the University accepted a gift which was later found to have been made to spite legitimate heirs. This estate was accepted prior to my term in office. It has been a satisfaction to me that in this case the distressed heirs on my request received compensation. During my regime the Regents refused to accept several bequests which would have caused undue hardship to members of a family.

The reasons which inspire gifts and bequests are occasionally unusual.

While I was still a young President, an alumnus who had become more or less accidentally a successful businessman appeared at my office with a proposal. He explained that he had never forgotten a course in the humanities which he had taken and that he would like to begin to make contributions toward the endowment of a professorship in that field. The amount then needed for an endowment was only a few hundred thousand dollars. After his visit and his initial contribution he returned to the University year after year, increasing the amounts which he was subscribing. On a later visit I told him that his contributions were far in excess of the amount originally thought sufficient. His reply was, "True, Mr. President, I must be enjoying the habit I have acquired."

Another case was very puzzling for years. I received a telephone call from a former judge who had become a trust officer in one of the large Detroit banks. He was evidently in some distress. He wanted me to talk to one of the bank's disgruntled depositors. I explained that I would like to accommodate him but did not see what I could do in a matter of the kind. The depositor was causing him considerable annoyance. He was critical of what the banks had been doing before and during the depression, and he wasn't quite sure they knew what they were doing after the depression. I could not help saying that possibly the client had something on his side. This didn't seem to be a satisfying observation, but it was finally arranged that I should talk to the man for whatever good it might do.

Very soon thereafter a tall, lean, austere man appeared, who sat down and began a long criticism of banks and bankers. Finally, after an hour-long lecture during which I was trying to discover what I could do to soothe his irritated feelings he remarked that he thought he would move to Ann Arbor. He asked me to recommend a real estate agent he could consult. This was moving rather fast. I countered with the suggestion that I give him a card to the Michigan Union. He could live there for a short period and take time to discover if he really would like to live in the city. He promptly accepted my invitation. I explained to him very carefully that under the rules he could only live in the Union as a guest for one month.

He not only stayed for the prescribed time, but refused to move thereafter. At the end of the school year he came to see me again to say that he was going east for the summer but would return in the fall. Furthermore, he expected to have his same room on his return. Before I could repeat that this was against the rules he added, "I am going to make out my will in favor of the University," and requested that I recommend a lawyer. This put a little different complexion on the matter. I recommended the University's firm of attorneys, and he made an appointment that day, after discussing at some length the best use to be made of his bequest.

The attorney soon called me to say that he was uncertain as to what he should do. He thought possibly there was an estate of about $200,000, but there might be much less. He was disturbed, however, for the prospective donor insisted that he, the attorney, witness the will and that the President of the University should be executor of the estate. Neither of us wanted these responsibilities. I called the gentleman and explained our position. He listened carefully and then said emphatically, "You will be the executor and the attorney will witness the will, or my money will go to another institution." Even if no more than $10 was involved I thought the University was as worthy of his support as any other institution I knew.

I called the attorney and proposed that we let the matter stand until fall, when the man was to return to Ann Arbor. He came back in the autumn, took his room in the Union, and refused to change his will in any particular. Hoping to do something about it sometime we did not argue the matter. Our paying guest lived in the Union for twelve years during which time we were unable to get any concessions about the conditions of his will. He continued to insist he would give the money to another university if we refused to serve as stipulated.

During the years he lived at the Union he became an interesting figure on the campus. He was always very reserved and gave the appearance of being in modest circumstances. The men students were kind to him, occasionally inviting him to dinner in a dormitory, probably thinking he would appreciate a free meal.

On returning to Ann Arbor from an extended alumni trip I was told that he was ill in the hospital. I sent word I would call on him the next day. During the night he passed away.

A few months before his death he had come to my office with a sizable stack of bank books in his hand. He was on his way to put them in a safety deposit box in the bank, and he remarked, as he had on previous occasions, that in case of his death I should find his papers including his will in his box. Upon being informed of his death I had an acting executor appointed.

After the proper preliminaries, the acting executor examined the safety deposit box and found bank books representing numerous eastern banks, in each of which was a small deposit. There was some stock, but in addition a large number of receipts for which there was no stock. There was no will. In going through his room at the Union where we expected to find his will, since it was not in the box, we failed to find either more stock or the will.

We informed some distant relatives of his death, and they replied that they had no interest in the matter. They knew the estate was to be left to the University, and they understood he had been ruined in the depression. We could bury the man ourselves. When it turned out, however, that the will could not be found the relatives immediately appeared on the scene.

The acting executor was as disturbed as I was. There was apparently little money, although many stock and dividend receipts. The will could not be found. Finally, after several days of careful search we again went through his room. We could not believe the will had been destroyed, and there was a chest of family heirlooms missing. This time the assistant manager of the Union accompanied the searchers. He remarked finally, "I see you have been through the room, taken up the carpet, ransacked the desks, and gone through this closet, but how about the other closet?" It then developed there were two closets in the room—one concealed behind a dresser. When this closet was opened we found it stacked with envelopes, some of them with letters enclosed, others with advertisements. Finally, wrapped up with some advertising material, we found the lost will and well over a million dollars in securities, many of them dating years back, which had never been converted into later issues.

I recalled then that the donor had told me that wills had on some occasions disappeared even from safety deposit boxes. The careful old gentleman had made sure that his will would ultimately be found. Furthermore, to insure that the University could not be accused of influencing him, he had attached to his last will an old one which stipulated simply that it was his intention to leave his money to the University.

The nicest thing about this episode was that in the desk of this benefactor, written several times on the backs of old envelopes and scraps of paper, was this sentence: "The more I see of Michigan students, the more pleased I am that my estate is going to the University of Michigan."

On a certain bright spring morning I was visited by an alumnus who had done much for the University. He said he had a proposal to make if I had a pet University project I would like to promote. I assured him I had several—for what college president has ever been in want of one or more projects needing support? He then outlined his proposal. He believed, as I did, that donors should make their contributions while they were living. His sister had fallen heir to a large fortune. He wanted to propose to her that she make a substantial gift to the University rather than leave a bequest to the institution. He suggested I write her a letter outlining the project I had in mind. He was sure that she would tell him of my letter, of which he was supposed to know nothing. When asked for his advice, he would urge her to come to Ann Arbor for further details or ask me to visit her.

After a few days she answered my letter, stating that she would call on me. In due time she was ushered into my office, accompanied by an elderly companion. The only remark made was that she had come to learn more of what I had in mind. I outlined the project with no evidence of any interest on the part of either one of the ladies. I tried to develop some of the details hoping some phase of the project would attract her interest. After a while with no encouragement I ran out of words. At that point both ladies rose and the prospective donor said, "I am not interested." Both of them walked out. I just had time to wish them a pleasant journey home. I hope I was sincere.

About a month later as I entered the office one morning, my secretary greeted me by asking, "How is your heart this morning?" Knowing that she was a serious young person I was rather surprised at the question. I assured her that as far as I knew my heart was perfectly sound. She replied, "It had better be when you see what is on your desk." On top of the morning mail was an envelope enclosing a million dollars from the lady, with no indication of any kind as to how she expected it to be used! I immediately called her brother, knowing he would be pleased and told him I would send her an acknowledgment immediately. He quickly informed me that under no circumstances must I thank her for the gift. "If you do, she is quite liable to cancel the check, for she resents any expression of appreciation for what she does." This episode marked the beginning of the Institute for Human Adjustment.

On another equally memorable occasion I had a call from a devoted alumnus, who had just arrived in Ann Arbor, asking for an interview. I told him I would be glad to see him in the office or to visit him in his temporary quarters, but our conversation would probably be more satisfactory if he came to the house that evening. He preferred to do that. The first thing he said on arrival was that he wanted to add to the resources of the University and would like to do it while he might have some pleasure in the use being made of his gift. He had in mind something which would make an impression on the students that would remain with them through the years. He preferred a contribution of aesthetic significance.

I told him I had regretted that a project of the alumni to erect a campanile with a set of chimes as a memorial to President Burton had failed. It was my thought that the University needed a set of bells and asked if this would please him. He said it was one thing he had had in mind. If I agreed we would settle on this campus feature.

He then wanted to know how much a set of bells would cost, where they could be made, and how long it would take to get them cast. I was out of my depth. I could only tell him I knew the head of the great Croyden Bell Foundry in England. I could write to him but possibly in the meantime we could get some needed information from the dean of the School of Music. He then told me he was ill, "living on borrowed time," and wanted no delay. I called the dean—I fear, getting him out of bed. He gave us a list of the sizes of the several sets of bells that had been made. We agreed we did not want electrical chimes. The donor desired to have the largest set that could be played manually.

The Dean offered to write the next day for costs and for the time that would be needed to cast the bells. This would not do. There was a transatlantic telephone. The firm should be called immediately. Fortunately, we were able to make the proper connections, and in the small hours of the morning the donor had the information he desired and had placed an order.

The next morning when he called me I immediately inquired about his health. He assured me that he had not slept so well for years. Before retiring, he had called his secretary and had her arrange to set aside the funds for the project.

At that point I began to realize I had a problem. There were tons of bells being cast in England for shipment on an uncertain date, but what were we going to do with them after they arrived? I consulted an architect who had had much to do with campus planning. We considered a number of plans such as putting a tower on the Michigan Union or some other existing building. The architect proposed a tower in the middle of the original campus. This did not seem an appropriate location. We finally agreed that if we could build a tower we should place it near Hill Auditorium in an area that at the time the

Regents had agreed would be the site for the future development of the School of Music.

We still, however, had to get funds for the structure. In desperation I decided to try a method of fund-raising that had been used successfully through the years in the construction of Old-World cathedrals. I announced to the residents of Ann Arbor, friends, and alumni that we would accept voluntary contributions both in money and in kind. The results were heartwarming. We had gifts of gravel, cement, hardware, and other building materials from local citizens. Contributions in cash ranged from two or three dollars to five thousand dollars. The tower went up rapidly.

The bell chamber was completed, but the building was far from finished when I was called by the Ann Arbor paper and informed that the bells were coming down Washtenaw Avenue on a fleet of trucks. I was aghast. I had not been informed of the shipment, and no arrangements had been made for installing the bells. I called the Engineering College for suggestions and was promptly told of one of our alumni in Detroit who was a specialist on heavy construction. I telephoned him and within a few hours his men and equipment had arrived and installed the bells.

If it is true, as is being said so often today, that tension is hard on the human system I must have aged considerably during this experience. One lasting satisfaction I had from it. The donor lived for several years, and I often saw him resting on a bench on the campus, listening to the chimes or the booming of the big bell (which I always called "Big Charley") as it counted off the hours.

This was one of the two times when I felt compelled to make a general appeal for funds.

As is well known but seldom admitted, some college presidents, like some ministers, are engaged as money-raisers. I hold these men in no disrespect. I was never able to understand, however, how one person could serve a university successfully in the combined roles of publicity agent, fund raiser, and head-master. At least I early discovered my own limitations in this respect and was made painfully aware of them in the campaign to raise funds for the Phoenix Project.

The history of this project is well known. Initiated by a student committee as a war memorial, and upon the suggestion of an alumnus, it quickly caught the imagination of both students and faculties. When general agreement was reached that the memorial should be a ten-year research program in the peacetime uses of atomic energy, the committee brought the proposal to me. I pointed out to them the large amount of money involved, how little the scientists actually knew about the potentialities of the newly released force, and the difficulty in describing such an unexplored field to practical-minded people. Their enthusiasm was unabated. They had talked with members of our faculty. The potentialities existed, although they had not been demonstrated. The estimated cost of a ten-year program was conservative. They knew that presentations to possible donors would have to be taken as "the substance of things hoped for, the evidence of things not seen." I finally asked what I should do. The chairman replied promptly: "Dr. Ruthven, we want you to get on your horse, ride out, and sell the Phoenix Project."

Later, when we suggested it might be easier to explain if the memorial was given a different name, we met firm opposition. If people didn't grasp the significance of the term Phoenix they could consult the dictionary. Some people didn't, and I received inquiries as to the reasons why the University planned to establish a research center in Phoenix, Arizona.

In view of the magnitude of the project and in the desire to obtain a broad participation by the alumni, it was decided to enlist the services of a professional firm of fund raisers. This was the first time, I believe, the University had employed this method of obtaining financial aid. The experience was also a new one for me. The decision proved wise.

I naively assumed that it was the business of fund raisers to raise funds. I soon learned that their task was to organize and direct the campaign; mine was to talk with individuals and speak at meetings of committees, alumni dinners, news conferences, and, when it could be arranged, over the radio. It was a strenuous life, necessitating much travel and many absences from the University. I found it hard to prepare appeals for funds on the basis of possibilities alone. The reporters were less reluctant than I to exercise their imagination. Occasionally, I returned to the campus to find our scientists upset over a news report in which a reporter had changed some possibility I had expressed into a prediction. In this campaign we naturally received less aid from our scholars than we did from industrialists accustomed to looking for, and taking, chances on potentialities.

In my pilgrim's progress on this mission, I was usually accompanied by two representatives of the professional organization. They preceded me to each stop and arranged for meetings and publicity. Association with these men was very pleasant, but even with their able assistance the trips were tiring, consisting usually of one-night stands. Also, I never knew what reception they and the alumni had arranged for me. In Tucson, we were greeted by the "Vigilantes," a gun-shooting organization. In Oregon I was sworn in as a deputy sheriff and a member of a sheriff's posse. By the governor I was given a commission as admiral in the Nebraska Navy, by the governor of Iowa I was awarded the Order of the Plow, and on the order of the governor of Wyoming Mrs. Ruthven and I were met at the train and transported to the capitol by stagecoach. Here and there I received a ten-gallon hat, keys to the city, or some other token of interest in my visit. Each one of these "honors" required an impromptu acknowledgment. Amusing as were these publicity "stunts" they served to advertise the project. The most difficult part of the campaign, however, was the necessity on each occasion of varying the presentations of the subject to suit the audience.

On the whole, the alumni were responsive, even when scientific terms were used which were as yet not in general use. The attitude of many of them was expressed by a former student when he remarked: "I don't know an isotope from a heliotrope, but if the University wants this project, I am for it." A number of corporations made generous contributions. The goal of the campaign was exceeded.

Viewed from this distance in time, it seems to me that the effort could not have failed. The appeal of student interest, the spirit of the alumni, the hard work of the alumni leaders, the efficiency of the professional staff, and the growing appreciation of the importance of the project insured success.

I have had but one regret. If the researches proved as significant as expected, and they have, by the end of the ten-year plan the University should have assumed much of the cost of continuing the investigations. As one of the most effective of the alumni leaders observed: "This campaign should be a one-shot affair. The University cannot afford to kill off its alumni every ten years for their golden eggs."

My regret now is that the real memorial gives promise of losing its identity, leaving behind only a building. This was just what the founders did not want to happen.

I was sometimes asked how I justified the acceptance of gifts to the University from persons with somewhat less than lily-white reputations. I had two stock answers: "The only trouble with tainted gift money is usually t'ain't enough," or as my grandmother said when the saloon-keeper offered her a contribution to the W.C.T.U., "I believe in taking from the devil and giving to the Lord."

It is common knowledge that gifts of money to universities and colleges come in different forms. Fortunately, I did not have to consider any that were made with the understanding that the University would secure the additional amount needed for a project. It always struck me as quite unfair, if not sadistic, for a would-be donor to place university officials under an obligation to solicit matching funds. Many college presidents have been forced into this embarrassing and time-consuming business. To one would-be donor of such a contingency gift I commented, "You are proposing that someone else help pay for your baby."

Gifts made with the provision that the donor's name be prominently associated with the project never seemed to me objectionable. I have often urged donors to permit use of their names. Surely benefactors no less than parents are deserving of credit.

The offer of a gift can prove embarrassing when the donor of a building insists on his own designs. The University has to my knowledge only two examples of this nature. One of these caused some trouble. The man who gave the Law Quadrangle supervised every detail of arrangement and design. This should have caused little embarrassment because there were only two activities to be performed in these buildings—the teaching of law and legal research. The donor was a distinguished lawyer, and the architects were well-qualified. I was concerned with the one part of the project, however, which caused some turmoil.

In building the library and the classroom building for the Law School the donor insisted that the faculty rooms in the library should be used by the staff members only for study. Other business was to be carried on in offices in the classroom building. To my predecessor and the dean of the School this provision was unsatisfactory as a matter of principle. As a result the construction of the classroom building was delayed. It was the contention of the President and the dean that the donor should make no stipulation as to the use of the two buildings. When I came into office the dispute seemed to me to make little sense. What the donor obviously had in mind—thinking back to his school days at Michigan—was that the law faculty should not use the library rooms for the practice of law! Of course the era in which professors practiced law on the side had long passed, and in my opinion the proviso prescribed by the donor meant nothing in our time.

A little-known episode occurred in the course of constructing the Law Quadrangle. The architects had designed and had carved small stone gargoyles in one of the passages in the Law Club. The heads portrayed certain members of the staff, including a few the donor did not like. When he saw the figures in a photograph he ordered the heads knocked off those representing men who had offended him. Years later when most of the cast of this little drama had left the scene, the contractor asked if I would like to have the heads restored. It seemed to me that the little monsters should remain decapitated as a part of the record.

I thoroughly agreed that no gift of buildings should be accepted with embarrassing restrictions as to design and function. Fortunately, I had little difficulty in convincing donors that our faculties knew best the facilities which they would need in their work and should participate in the planning of new buildings. I had good reason for this point of view long before I became President. For some time in my student career at another university I had to carry on my studies in a beautiful building which would have made a good monastery or a convenient place for studies in the humanities but was inconvenient as a place in which to pursue scientific investigations.

The story of the Rackham Building on the Ann Arbor campus should be told if for no other reason than to answer a criticism of its luxuriousness voiced by some at the time of its completion. Naturally, some would have preferred a more simple building and a larger endowment. The choice was not ours to make.

The late Horace H. Rackham, a Michigan alumnus, was a Detroit lawyer who, during his lifetime and always strictly anonymously, financed archeological work of the University in the Near East, particularly in Egypt, and in the Philippines. On his death the residue of his estate after special bequests had been satisfied was administered by a foundation for philanthropic and educational purposes.

Shortly after the Rackham Foundation was organized the trustees asked me for suggestions as to how they should operate the trust. I advised them to visit other foundations to learn of their experiences.

After making these visits the chairman of the board reported that the older foundations had frankly admitted the mistakes they had made. This was helpful. They had also suggested that, since they had now learned by experience how best to perform their functions, the Rackham funds might safely be placed in their custody. As the chairman of the Rackham Foundation put it: "We decided we would make our own mistakes."

As a beginning the trustees asked me to suggest a University project which would require funds to the amount of approximately $150,000 to $500,000. At the time the Graduate School was inadequately housed and inadequately financed. I could think of no more important needs. In a few days I outlined a proposal the estimated original cost of which would be about $5,000,000. The Foundation would erect a building for the school and provide an endowment for research. The University would designate the school as the Horace H. Rackham School of Graduate Studies. Further, it was suggested that the Foundation consider providing special funds for research.

The trustees of the Foundation promptly accepted the proposal with one modification. They would acquire the land and erect and equip a monumental building. The cost of the building and equipment would not affect the amount of the endowment. The site and the interior plans would be subject to the approval of the University. During the course of the planning and construction at no point were questions raised by the trustees as to the use to be made of the building or as to the arrangement of the space required by the University.

The University Extension Center in Detroit was also a gift of the Rackham Foundation. A grant had been made to the Engineering Society of Detroit for a building, but the appropriation was not large enough to provide for all of the needs of that organization. When I learned of this situation I proposed to the Foundation that funds be made available to the University for a much-needed Extension Center in Detroit and suggested a plan designed to benefit both institutions: a site adjoining the plot owned by the Engineering Society to be purchased as a University Extension Center, the two buildings to be owned separately, and to be united by a foyer, auditorium, and other facilities for joint use. The plan was quickly approved by the Foundation, the Society, and the University. The marriage has been a harmonious one.

The campus of the University of Michigan has sometimes been called an architectural museum. This is a misuse of the term "museum." In my opinion the variety of architecture on the campus is a clear indication that the buildings have been for the most part designed to meet the uses which they were to serve. The Law School could not be well housed in the Medical or Natural Science buildings, and certainly the Medical School or biological departments would be greatly handicapped if confined within the buildings of our Law School. For many years the method for planning buildings has been to have the faculties specify their needs and then to find architects to design a covering for them.

THE ALUMNI

I was an alumnus President, and thus had a double incentive to know and keep close to former students. It has been a Michigan tradition that the alumni constitute a fourth arm of the University. At least I could not subscribe to the statement of a president of another institution that after commencement he did not want to see the graduates again until they returned with a check. A close association maintained through the years proved rewarding, revealing, and sometimes disappointing. It led to a rough and ready classification of alumni into ten categories:

Those who have diplomas and those who do not.

Those who have achieved "success" and those who have been satisfied to be good citizens.

Those who appreciate what the University gave them and those who have convinced themselves that any success they may have had has been solely the product of their own native abilities and efforts.

Those interested in the major objectives of institutions of higher learning and those whose principal concern is with the sideshows.

Those who feel they should be of service to their alma mater and those who contend that they discharged their responsibilities when they paid their tuition.

I found I could live with, work with, and enjoy most of our alumni. It was impossible, however, not to be irritated at times with those who, having paid only a part of the cost of their education, would recognize no further obligation to their school—financial or otherwise. Especially annoying were those who, having achieved "success," had convinced themselves that they were "self-made."

She is an attractive, active alumna, married and with an interesting little family. I am sure that only she and I know that she does not have a diploma. She failed in her last semester's work, but was not daunted. She sent out invitations to commencement, rented a cap and gown, marched in the procession, and received congratulations from friends and relatives. I shall not give her away.

With my young son I was resting from the routine of conferences, individual and committee, by studying reptiles in the wildest part of the desert. The most comfortable way of returning to civilization was to journey to a watering stop, some seventy miles away, and try to induce the conductor of a transcontinental limited train to open his heart and a car door. The train rolled to a stop, but the cars remained closed. The conductor, watch in hand, was adamant. Rules were rules. It was not a scheduled station stop. A freight would be along sometime, and he strolled away.

Someone was about to lose face, but prestige was saved. Along the train came a division superintendent. It evidently occurred to him as a possibility that the tramps might not be what they seemed. Could the travelers identify themselves? They could and would. As the University was mentioned, the conductor, just within earshot, whirled and threw open a door.

"Hurry and get aboard, we are starting."

"Have you seats for them?" asked the astonished superintendent.

"Seats, hell! They can have the whole train. I belong to the class of '88."

My son insists that this was the time when he was most impressed by his father's position.

The luncheon arranged by the alumni was late. With apologies the hosts explained that one of their number was detained. They hesitated to gather at the festive board until he arrived. He was a great man in the city and state, an eminent jurist, and a judge in a high court. I was hungry but still amiable when his honor appeared, dignified but unhurried.

As salutations were exchanged, it slowly dawned on me that I was being scrutinized closely. The judge was evidently not at ease. When introduced he seemed uncertain about something. Apparently, he wanted to make a comment or ask a question and was not quite certain that he could or should.

Finally, the great one decided on the indirect approach. He asked if universities ever withdrew degrees. It is a stock joke among alumni, and there is a stock reply: "There is no recorded case, but graduates should be good or it might sometime be done." The next question was more specific: "What would happen if an institution discovered after a lapse of years that a former student had gained admission under false pretenses?" The answer again was easy. If the crooked student had become a respected and sufficiently distinguished citizen, the university authorities might be inclined to make an honest man of him by giving him an honorary degree.

The eminent judge looked relieved that the matter could be discussed so pleasantly. His conscience had evidently been troubling him, and he wanted to make confession. He proceeded with his story.

He had graduated from high school a year before his brother, with grades which would not allow him to enter the University. He rusticated for a year and then applied for admission on the more satisfactory record of his brother. The matter of names was easily handled. He was Alexander Blackstone Smith. His brother was Blaine Andrew Smith. As a freshman he registered as B. Andrew Smith. As a sophomore he became Andrew B. Smith. When he was made a junior, he changed his cognomen to A. Blackstone Smith. Finally, as a senior he was born again Alexander Blackstone Smith, and his diploma was thus inscribed. The registrars were easy in his day.

With apprehension, but evidently relieved that the horrid deed had been acknowledged, the judge became the culprit at the bar of justice awaiting his sentence.

The father confessor tried to keep a straight face and to adopt a judicial manner. How were his grades in college? They were excellent. What happened to the brother? He had entered another law school, graduated with honors, and was now on the bench in another state. Then came the verdict delivered in, what was hoped, pontifical tones:

"My son, I give you absolution. Go and sin no more."

It was my endeavor always to be of service to the alumni. But even though I was not averse to stretching or even breaking a rule now and then, there were alumni problems which I could not solve.

The alumnus was an active member of a local club and a respected professional man. There was no diploma in his office. At club roll call he avoided giving his class. He confided his dilemma to Mrs. Ruthven, and gained an ally. He had for some reason, not revealed to me, entered college and graduated under an assumed name. I wanted the University to issue a new diploma under his own name, but the Regents were adamant. I still think this should have been done in spite of the rules.

The "loyalty" of Michigan alumni is traditional. They join the local clubs and return to the campus for class reunions and general alumni meetings in respectable numbers. Their individual gifts have been important. Every president of the University has appreciated these expressions of interest by former students. It must be admitted, however, that this so-called "Michigan spirit" has not been as effective in promoting the welfare of the University as it might have been with better channels of communication between the graduate and his school. Two reasons why a larger measure of alumni co-operation has not been received, it seems to me, are the confusion of aims and the cumbersome organization in the central office of the Alumni Association.

One guiding concept of the Association has been that it should be a loose organization of primarily social clubs. The clubs are to stimulate local interest in the University and foster a spirit of unity among the members. Presumably, they should also serve as centers of information about the University for the alumni and as a means of acquainting the University with alumni thinking. Above all, the clubs should not be money-raising units if the Association continues to remain an independent corporation.

This concept is good as far as it goes, but it does not, in practice, go far enough to be of the greatest possible service, either to the alumni or the University. Obviously, the alumni cannot be sufficiently informed through sporadic visits of University representatives to their clubs to serve as interpreters of University policies and practices or advisers to the University on alumni problems. Furthermore, the semiannual meetings in Ann Arbor of the district directors can do little to improve the communications problem.

Another school of thought would have the Association be, in important part, an independent fund-raising organization, deriving its operating expenses from fees and a percentage of gifts to the University. This plan has the shortcomings of the first one together with other faults. Gifts made to the University are tax-free. For this and other reasons it is doubtful that many donors, including alumni, would be willing to have a part of their contributions for specific University purposes—which could be made directly and more legitimately to the Board of Regents—diverted to Association support. Again, many alumni are not and never will be members of clubs. The problem of financial support and the use of gift funds is solely a responsibility of the University. The opportunity to assist the institution is a privilege and should be so regarded. Finally, who can doubt that club memberhips, difficult as they are to maintain, would be discouraged by placing their reason for existence on the willingness of members to pay.

In an attempt to improve means of communication between the alumni and the University, I asked the Regents to approve the appointment of a director of Alumni Relations to work closely with the general secretary of the Association. Under his direction, we created an alumni advisory council composed of members selected from the different districts and meeting each year in Ann Arbor at times when there were no special diversions. The members were asked in advance of the meetings to select topics for discussion, but matters considered were not limited to these suggestions. The meetings, extending continuously over a day or two, were most interesting and helpful. The questions were searching, and the answers by informed members of the administrative staff and faculties were at all times full and frank. When the members of the council returned to their districts, they attended club meetings in their areas to report on the information received.

Unfortunately, this experiment had to be discontinued during the war and was not revived. In its place, however, as an outgrowth of the Phoenix Project, the Development Council was formed, which is proving to be not only an effective fund-raising agency but also a channel of communication between the University and its former students.

The term "alumni giving" is often heard in university circles. Seldom if ever in state schools has it reflected a very general concern for the welfare of higher education on the part of former students. Aside from the too general feeling that public education, being the responsibility of the state, does not need the individual support of its beneficiaries there are to my knowledge other reasons for the failure of Michigan alumni to give active support to the University.

The experiences of the Phoenix campaign demonstrated that alumni interest could be stimulated and maintained by a program of annual giving. For too long we had been regrettably slow to act on the lesson read to mankind centuries ago: "Where your treasure is, there will your heart be." The Michigan Alumni Fund established by the Development Council bids fair to be successful in improving alumni relations.

Financial support from alumni and other benefactors, it is sometimes argued, could in the long run weaken the responsibility of the state for the college education of its youth. This contention (or excuse) makes little real sense. Gifts to state schools are customarily for purposes for which the legislature could not be expected to provide. As I now cheerfully admit, I never encouraged "undesignated" contributions. I encouraged donors to attach one "string" to gifts—the stipulation that they should be used for a specific purpose or for a nearly allied purpose if or when the original one no longer existed.

Alumni interest can and should mean more than the giving of financial support, important as this is. It should include a willingness on the part of the individual to serve as an informed interpreter of the activities of his university and of the importance of higher education. In our society it is the alumni who have the responsibility and should be best able to project an undistorted image of our institutions of higher learning.

Finally, it appears to me that in this area the avenue of communication should really be a two-way street. In short, if an alumni association is effective it should have generous financial support from the university which it serves.

In my early years as President I summarized my views on alumni relations in a brief creed:

"We believe that the student should be trained as an Alumnus from matriculation; he enrolls in the University for life and for better or worse he will always remain an integral part of the institution.

"We believe that the relations between the alumnus and his University should be beneficial to both, and that the mutual assistance provided by the graduates and by the institution should be limited only by their powers for service.

"We believe that to the person who has obtained what he should from his alma mater, Michigan is the actual expression of a practical idealism—government, religion, and state supported education being inseparable—; and

"We believe that to the University the alumnus is a member of a brotherhood bound by the spiritual tie of faith in the ideals of education."

On my retirement the alumni by action of the Board of Directors of the Association conferred on me the title of Dean of Alumni. This honor I prize highly.

PENULTIMATE THOUGHTS

The official date of my retirement was June 30. Since my successor was not to arrive until September, I was asked by the Regents to continue in office during the summer. At this time certain questions came to mind which I suspect come to others on the eve of retirement.

Had I been wise in allowing my career to be changed in mid-course? My first college Latin teacher in a letter explained in nonbiological language the futility of considering this question: The same organism in the same environment when subjected to the same stimulus will always react in the same way.

In what successes could I take pride? I quickly decided it would be best not to attempt to answer this query. Future generations would make the decisions. Whatever achievements may be credited to my regime, I hope they will be understood to have been in no small part due to the loyalty and wisdom of my associates.

What mistakes and failures should I regret? I freely admit to some errors in judgment. These have been corrected or will be in time. I do not apologize for them. After all, "If things were done twice all would be wise." I will always regret three failures: my inability to limit the size of the University, to halt increases in student fees, and to work out with my colleagues and the legislature a sensible method of allocating state funds for the support of higher education.

What compensation did I find in administration for the associated trials and tribulations? This question was asked in different forms by a number of interested friends. I can answer without hesitation, and I believe objectively. The major reward was a feeling of satisfaction that I was helping to maintain a favorable environment for students and staff members. This, I suppose, was to be expected—a naturalist has profound regard for the influence of the environment on living things.

Why in this day and age does it continue to be necessary to explain to parents and taxpayers the objectives and importance of their institutions of higher learning? I respectfully refuse to answer this question on the grounds that my comments might be construed as libelous.

President Tappan drew an accurate sketch of a university as a group of scholars devoted to the instruction of youth and the increase of knowledge. His successors, especially President Angell and President Hutchins, elaborated this concept without changing its meaning, and the true image of the University of Michigan today is that envisaged by its first great presidents:

A University is an *old thing*; and the principle of it is as clear as noonday. University development keeps pace with the advance of knowledge. It advances knowledge and spreads itself necessarily with this advance; but the principle and the forms are ever essentially the same.

Surely, even the so-called "man-on-the-street" should in the course of almost one hundred years have come to an understanding of his highest schools.

Retirement

Before you think of retiring from the world be sure you are fit for retirement.

THE SIXTH REBIRTH

IT HAS BEEN my opinion that men should retire to live, not to die. This accounts for the interest I have taken in the Institute for Human Adjustment and in the general field of geriatrics. As President I observed men capable of continuing productive lives retire to a frustrating and sometimes even bitter existence. As one commentator has observed: "Many men dive into retirement and are amazed to find no water in the pool."

My first effort to improve the conditions of retirement for the staff was to have the Regents grant the faculty a one-year voluntary retirement furlough at age sixty-nine. This should, it seemed to me, ease the shock of adjustment to what for many teachers and scholars will be a radically new life.

The most important task that faced my administration in this area was to effect improvements in our retirement plan for the academic staff and the formulation of a similar plan for the nonacademic employees. These were made thanks largely to the assistance of the staff.

After the University has done all it can there remains much for the person to do for himself if he is to lead a satisfying life after he is relieved of the responsibilities of whatever position he has held. It frequently has been emphasized, especially in recent years, that one should plan early for retirement and choose a worthwhile occupation for the later years, such as scholarly, business, professional, or creative work in one of the arts. This would seem to be evident.

I began early to plan for the termination of my services with the University. I had from boyhood an interest in horses. One of my grandfathers raised harness horses, my father raised Shires, and ever since I had my first horse, at eight years of age, I enjoyed handling them. Again, as a biologist the heredity and variations in the species presented an interesting field of study. After I became President, the Regents informed me that I would have to give up my expeditions to the tropics. (The only answer I received to my protest was: "The selection of a university president is an onerous, irksome and frustrating job.") Not being interested in golf, hunting, fishing, or other sports I decided it was a good time to begin preparation for retirement by attempting to revive an old and distinguished breed of horses which at one time was fast disappearing.

I first became acquainted with the Morgan horse when as a boy I saw these beautiful animals on some of the covered wagons going West with easterners who were helping to open certain Indian reservations. I decided to begin studies of this breed, acquired two registered mares and a stallion from Vermont, and began experimental breeding. This has been an absorbing business which has now brought into complete cycle one of my long-time interests.

Visitor: "I understand Dr. Ruthven has retired. I would like to see him. Where is he?"

Tex (manager of Stanerigg for almost twenty-five years): "I have him back where he started. He is working in the stable."

Finally, at the end of my period of active service I was appointed consultant to the newly established Development Council of the University and accepted directorships on the boards of the Ann Arbor Trust Company and the Lincoln National Life Insurance Company. These activities have opened new vistas of life—its problems and responsibilities. Probably most importantly, this period has materially enlarged my circle of busy and interesting associates. My former friends and acquaintances have been reshuffled. Some of the former have slipped into other orbits. Some previous acquaintances have become close friends.

One question too often asked irritates me, "Are you having a good rest?" To my way of thinking six to eight hours of sleep are enough rest for any healthy adult. To spend more time on one's downy cot or otherwise doing nothing worthwhile is sheer indolence.

Life for me is pleasant, rewarding, often amusing, and sometimes exciting. What more could one desire?